PRAISE

"*Garden to G*...
than chase do...
roadside berries...
weeds. This is a...
cocktail, one that...
the fruits and her...
improvisational sp...
you'll never look at...
 — Amy Stewart, *New*...

"There has always b...
is *thoughtful*. Though...
detail in his work. *Gard*...
and the ingredients it t...

"If the cocktail renaissan...
about people rediscovering...
etc. from the past, and the...
new era of originality and c...
one like Mike to show us wha...
—Matt T...

"I'm always drawn to people w...
they do. Mike Wolf is one of the...
dive into the world of gardening...
ite pastimes. When I grab a sea...
knowing that I'm in great hands,...
conversation! With this book, the...
great vibes on every page!"

"Mike Wolf is among the best barte...
smart, creative, and most importantly...
have for anyone trying to build upon...
utilize farmed and foraged ingredients...
drinks. Also - Brian Baxter's watercolors...
— Jo...

GARDEN

to

GLASS

Mike Wolf

Turner Publishing Company
Nashville, Tennessee
www.turnerpublishing.com

Garden to Glass: Grow Your Drinks from the Ground Up

Cover design: Bryce McCloud
Book design: Stacy Wakefield Forte
Illustrations: Brian Baxter
Illustrations: Jess Machen
Photography: Peter Frank Edwards

Library of Congress Cataloging-in-Publication Data available upon request

9781684422098 Paperback
9781684422081 Hardcover
9781684422104 Ebook

Printed in the United States of America
17 18 19 20 10 9 8 7 6 5 4 3 2 1

DEDICATION

To Kate, Leila, Henry, Boone, June
and the memory of Merle

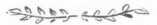

CONTENTS

FOREWORD

Mike Wolf was one of my first hires when I came to Nashville, Tennessee to open Husk. My hiring process tends to be an ardent one. I can tell pretty quickly when someone is going to fit into our culture by how many times they smile when I am rambling on about Southern food being amongst the best in the world. Mike was one of those interviews that stood out, and I hired him instantly. I wanted to work very closely with the bar team to ensure that what ended up in the glass matched the ethos of our cooking. My advice was to find the most vibrant and exquisite products each day, then do very little to them and make sure they sang. Mike had already been thinking in that direction, and I could see his face light up with curiosity and wonderment. As we embarked on the initial research and development for Husk Nashville's opening menu, I recall the relief I felt when I tasted Mike's first creations. I didn't have to worry about the beverage program anymore, because he was already thinking the way we do in the kitchen.

We built a large garden around the restaurant and made sure that the landscaping was mostly edible. My favorite herb, and most certainly one of my favorite smells, is lovage. On our opening menu I created a dish inspired by my mom's chicken and dumplings (one of the South's most iconic comfort foods). I added lovage to the dumplings and we had to plant a lot more in the garden to keep up. I recall going to the garden one day to pick some herbs and realized that most of the lovage from the day before was gone. "Morgan!

What happened to the lovage?" Morgan replied, "Mike is making something for his cocktail menu with it." I said, "Please inform him that if he wants to use that much lovage, he needs to grow it himself!" I was half-joking, but it didn't get translated to Mike that way. Before long he was coming to work with enormous bouquets of fresh herbs from his house and planting random things outside the back door of the restaurant bar. At one point, I was actually raiding his plants by the light of the moon after he had gone home. When you walked into the bar during service you were met with giant bundles of redbud flowers sitting in water, next to bunches of elderflowers and Queen Anne's lace. It appeared as though we hired a florist to just focus on the bar. It was exciting to collaborate with someone who was as inspired as I was by Mother Nature.

I always loved seeing Mike pop-in to the kitchen with his latest creation, presenting it on the pass the way a sous chef would present a new salad. "Chef, taste this and tell me what you think!" In *Garden to Glass* he showcases his alchemy with tinctures and potions that you can also make at home with herbs from your windowsill or dandelion from your front yard. After reading these pages you will start to see nature become your grocery store, and your back yard will likely be dug up to make room for more lovage before you know it.

SEAN BROCK

INTRODUCTION

It's funny how the simplest things can fall forward in life, like how a glance around the bar in a quick moment before service became the first domino that tumbled into the creation of this book. I remember a day at now-defunct Nashville cocktail bar Holland House, when we had run out of blackberries and we happened to have a very popular blackberry old fashioned on the menu. I mentioned how I had been riding my bike down at Shelby Park, an immense public park with greenways and wild spaces in East Nashville, and I noticed wild blackberries growing all over the place. When I suggested we just go down there and pick some, everybody looked at me like I was crazy. When I went to pick blackberries the next day, I noticed exotic flowers popping up all over the place that turned out to be wild passionflower and elderflower. It took a lot of research and cross-checking, but my curiosity only grew from there. A few years later, I was working at Rumours East, located in a charming bungalow in the historic Lockeland Springs neighborhood. In the backyard, we had a garden filled with herbs and vegetables that the chef, Hrant Arakelian, who has since moved on to open the amazing Lyra, used in his signature modern Middle Eastern food. I realized that it didn't take an entire farm's worth of ingredients to make a big difference in the quality of the drinks. I would cut a few herbs here and there to garnish a gimlet, and during the summer I would pick from the honeysuckle vine that filled the whole patio and garden area with its warm, floral perfume. The combination of lemon thyme and honeysuckle flowers sitting on top of the foam from a silky egg-white whiskey sour, was a turning point for me. The aroma was so intense. The drink was dynamic and complex, and I knew I was beginning a whole new journey.

Gardening is a lot like the bar and restaurant business. Just when you think you've got a handle on things, something unforeseen happens and you have a whole new set of problems on your hands. You think you've mastered one particular area only to discover you never really knew how much you thought you did. The more you know or come to learn, the more you realize you've been doing things wrong. But once you settle into the mindset that you're going to learn a little something new everyday, that obstacles are always waiting around the corner, that nature is unpredictable and wiser than you, then you realize that all these little mistakes you're making are the seeds falling in the dirt which will grow again—as wisdom in bloom. Gardening taught me that as things decay, they are merely setting the stage for rebirth. I've seen this happen with relationships, as well as restaurants and bars I've worked in that are no longer around, including the two I just mentioned. I've also seen it with plants, like a beloved patch of rhubarb I left behind at an old house we lived in. It was my ultimate signifier for spring, and an inspiration every year to get back out in the garden.

When I had the opportunity to open Husk in Nashville and jump-start the bar program there, I found people like Chef Sean Brock, Brian Baxter, Lisa Donovan, and Nate Leonard (many of whom contributed to this book) who all had an intense passion for ingredients, flavor, time-honored traditions, and bold new experimentation. We had an expansive on-site garden at Husk and as the months and years went on, we were constantly developing it, adding pockets of strange herbs to any corner of sunlight we could find. Many of them are still there today (Rory, have you watered the woodruff?) and the entire staff works to maintain the gardens. However, in a highly charged, chef-driven environment, it can be unwise for a bartender to stroll out into the garden and clip the best herbs and flowers for that night's service. Sometimes I'd find myself out in the garden and there'd be a knock on the glass from one of the sous chefs followed by the mostly good-natured side to side no-no-no finger-wagging as I inspected the borage flowers. So I began to focus more on what I could grow at home and experimented with playing with the rhythms of my own garden. To use dill flowers, I had to have the patience to grow them in stages and stagger their development, so I didn't use too much at once. Later I would realize that the huge hollow stems of a mature dill plant could be used for drink straws. I was constantly learning.

I also dove into the local flora and expanded our ingredient library to include some of the exotic botanicals and flowers which grow wild locally in and around Nashville. Elderflower, wild roses, honeysuckle, sumac, wild carrot, passion fruit, even simple things like red clover, violet, and the almighty dandelion, all added aromas and flavors to the drinks and showcased a diverse microclimate. My hope is that this book can help bartenders, beverage directors, home enthusiasts, and those interested in gardening, to expand their offerings and begin to cultivate their own ingredient libraries. When you've grown something yourself, harvested it in the morning after the dew has faded, and used it in a drink (or *fine*, a dish) the result is so much more dynamic than if that same ingredient came in off a truck from a different part of the country. One of my favorite moments working on the book came when I talked to Jeff Poppen, the Barefoot Farmer, and he said "Don't forget that your garden is part of something larger." He points out that it puts you in an interaction with the whole universe. So, go ahead and let your dandelions bloom. The bees, and your drinks, will thank you.

CHAPTER

1

THE COMMENCEMENT

Bitter Beginnings

I t was a Middle Tennessee summer day at Husk; the stage (and the tables) were set for an intricate 10-course meal in the converted old horse stables of the antebellum mansion on Rutledge Hill, a mile south of and overlooking the ever-changing skyline of downtown Nashville. For Chef Sean Brock, who moved to Nashville six years ago to open the second version of his famous Husk Restaurant in Charleston, South Carolina, these dinners, called the "Stables Workshop Series," were an opportunity to try new things, develop new techniques, and experiment with different flavor combinations. It was the beginning of a new artistic direction for him, continuing to focus on hyperlocal ingredients, though now with a minimalist aesthetic inspired by the food he had experienced throughout Japan. Since we were in the sweet spot of summer, before it got too hot and while the elderflower was still in bloom, the ingredients available for the dinner were voluminous. Flowering basils, squash perfectly in season, cucumber blossoms, the kind of overflowing baskets of perfect produce that would be cut like a Tarantino action scene and set to Vivaldi on "Chef's Table." I was tasked with developing non-alcoholic beverage pairings for the sophisticated dishes, using produce and herbs from the garden. As was common when working with Chef Brock, there was always something new to learn, and one thing in particular stood out.

Upon returning to the kitchen from the garden, Chef began infusing freshly cut tomato leaves into a sauce using an ISI charger, typically used for whipped cream or instantly infusing flavors into olive oil. I had never seen tomato leaves used in a recipe before, but the aroma of the leaves filling the kitchen that day reminded me of the herbs out in the garden that go so well with tomatoes: basil and parsley. I investigated this further, retreating back out into the garden to cut some tomato leaf along with basil and parsley. The aroma of the three ingredients together was a powerhouse of flavor affinity! I felt like I was transported to the kitchen of an Italian grandmother who's been toiling away on a twelve-hour sauce for a family feast deep in the hills of Tuscany. I used this flavor combination for a savory soda to pair with a crab and rice dish later in the meal. During that summer in the bar, I began using tomato leaves in elaborate European-style gin and tonic garnishes and would even sneak some tomato leaf into a pesto sauce I would make at home. It was discoveries like these that inspired me to expand my garden and to use as much of it as I could. When you have a garden, these are the kinds of discoveries that can change the way you cook—or, in our case, drink.

GETTING YOUR GARDEN STARTED

While I'd love to inspire you to overhaul some sunny spot in your yard and turn it into a diverse gardenscape overflowing with flowers, herbs, and vegetables, I would also encourage you to expand or contract your growing space to fit your needs. Start slow and build. Try new seeds, plants you've never heard of. You'll learn something new with every different plant you grow—and just when you think you've got a handle on things, you'll realize you forgot to fertilize, and your plants are changing color. It's quite all right, because like humans, plants are resilient. Many of the ingredients we'll focus on in this book are herbs, which are great plants to begin your gardening journey with. Herbs are generally easy to grow and can adapt to many different growing conditions. They'll also give you the confidence to try growing other things, from a large elderberry shrub to climbing and curling scarlet runner beans (whose flowers make for beautiful cocktail garnishes!). Cilantro, whose seeds are known as coriander, is a great example of an herb that is easy to grow. Just drop a few seeds on the ground, lightly push them into the dirt, spray a little water on them, and walk away. Within a week you'll see some cilantro beginning to grow.

I'm no master gardener, that's for sure. But my passion for plants and how they have shaped the drinks we enjoy, along with the possibilities they have opened up for me as a beverage professional, has helped keep me centered in a business that is always changing and keeping me on my toes (much like nature). Gardening, with all its trial and error, is a lot like any other time-honored endeavor, like baking or sewing. At some point, usually when frustration creeps in, you'll get that feeling of "I don't know what the hell I'm doing. I should just leave this to the professionals" (personally, baking totally put me down for the count). But just as there's nothing like a freshly baked loaf of bread, the benefits of growing your own ingredients are well worth all the effort. Take the everyday herb parsley, for example—specifically flat parsley, or Italian parsley. It's available in many different forms in the grocery store, from freeze-dried to packaged dried to fresh. Often, even at high-end markets with good organic produce, the fresh parsley will have just a faint aroma or no aroma at all. Go ahead, try it out. When you go to buy parsley, first shake it to wake it up a little, then bring it up to your nose and smell. If you get hit with a lively fresh parsley aroma, you've got a solid bunch in your hand. However, I've found that most parsley in markets and grocery stores just doesn't smell like anything at all.

Now try growing parsley in a large pot, or planted in the ground in your garden and given enough space to thrive. The aroma of freshly cut parsley will bowl you over with its pungent power. Anything you make with it, from roast chicken to chicken salad to beef stroganoff, will be immensely better with this freshly grown herb. And how else would you know the joys of parsley flowers? A flavor so complex and divine, like caviar of the garden, fit to sprinkle on anything from lemonade to a gin gimlet to ribeye to roasted potatoes. Growing parsley gives you four fresh options to use instead of two: you'll have the stem, leaves, root, and flower to choose from, instead of just the stem and leaves that were grown in another state, region, or in some cases, another country. Growing your own makes common herbs suddenly uncommon because they're so fresh and dynamic. You can cut a few stems to dry to use at Thanksgiving and come back a few weeks later to see that more parsley has grown back, stronger than ever. You'll be amazed at how the herbs and flowers you grow respond to your rhythms as a gardener. If you have one basil plant and seem to be cutting it often to use in pesto and all your summer daiquiris, it will shoot off in many different directions to try and keep up. If you don't seem to be cutting it that often, it will slow its pace and round out naturally.

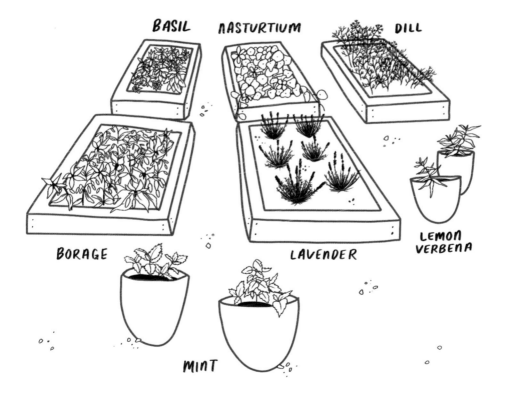

BASIL   NASTURTIUM   DILL

BORAGE   LAVENDER   LEMON VERBENA

MINT

WHEN PLANNING YOUR GARDEN, HERE ARE SOME KEY QUESTIONS TO KEEP IN MIND:

* How much sunshine is available in your growing space? Most of the plants you will grow will require between four and eight hours of direct or partial sunlight a day. Vegetables like tomatoes, peppers, and okra will need that hot late afternoon sun to fully mature and ripen. Many herbs love morning and mid-day sun and noticeably cringe with too much late-afternoon heat. If you live in an apartment building in an urban area and you have a balcony, keep an eye on how much and what kind of sunlight your balcony gets. Herbs can get along quite well with that fluttering part-shade, part-sun situation so common in leafy neighborhoods, where tree limbs dance around, throwing little flecks of sunlight on the ground below.

* Are there trees blocking too much of your sunshine? If so, a little tree maintenance, a necessary evil if you're a home-owner, can give you as much as two to three hours of extra sunlight, which could be the difference between thriving plants and sad plants.

* How much space do you have? If you'd like to start small— and some functional kitchen herb gardens can be as small as a corner of dirt that's 2 feet by 3 feet—it can be helpful to think about where and how you can expand your growing options. The patterns of the sun on your growing space will help you decide your options in terms of future expansion. It's good to think about this early because growing things can become addictive, and you'll always be looking for more growing space!

* Which growing zone are you in? There are nine zones in the United States, and where you are on the Hardiness Zone Map

can help you decide which plants you'll be able to grow. Many herbs are adaptive to different growing zones.

* What are your goals for your garden? If you're in the beverage industry, are you looking to provide mint for your bar for the whole summer? That would require you to give your mint plenty of space and time to grow and spread out (which mint loves to do). Is the goal to make bitters from your garden? That would require some diversity in what you plant. Are you interested in growing herbs that are hard to find from your suppliers? Are you just growing for garnish?

* What is already available in your area? If you find yourself at markets in the summer and fall perusing the local bounty, what is easy for you to source there, and what vegetables or herbs are harder to find? This can help you narrow the scope of your garden. For example, squash is everywhere in the markets near my home of Nashville, Tennessee. My friends from White Squirrel Farm (page 203) in Bethpage, who grow amazing vegetables and have helped feed my family for years, grow all kinds of delicious squash. But growing squash on my own is the only way to have squash blossoms on hand, since they are typically not sold in stores and only rarely sold in markets, fetching high prices when they do appear. Fortunately, the squash bores, the nasty pests who bore into my squash on the sly and destroy it before they can be detected, usually solve that problem for me.

* Will you be planting things in the ground, in containers, or in raised beds? If you'll be using your own soil, you can take a sample to get tested at a local agricultural center. This test can help ascertain which nutrients you may need to add to your soil to encourage plant health. Raised beds make things a little easier, as you'll be bringing in dirt and potting soil that will be tailor-made for growing things. If you have limited

HARDINESS
ZONE MAP

Temp (F)	Zone	Temp (C)
-60 to -55	1a	-51.1 to -48.3
-55 to -50	1b	-48.3 to -45.6
-50 to -45	2a	-45.6 to -42.8
-45 to -40	2b	-42.8 to -40
-40 to -35	3a	-40 to -37.2
-35 to -30	3b	-37.2 to -34.4
-30 to -25	4a	-34.4 to -31.7
-25 to -20	4b	-31.7 to -28.9
-20 to -15	5a	-28.9 to -26.1
-15 to -10	5b	-26.1 to -23.3
-10 to -5	6a	-23.3 to -20.6
-5 to 0	6b	-20.6 to -17.8
0 to 5	7a	-17.8 to -15
5 to 10	7b	-15 to -12.2
10 to 15	8a	-12.2 to -9.4
15 to 20	8b	-9.4 to -6.7
20 to 25	9a	-6.7 to -3.9
25 to 30	9b	-3.9 to -1.1
30 to 35	10a	-1.1 to 1.7
35 to 40	10b	1.7 to 4.4
40 to 45	11a	4.4 to 7.2
45 to 50	11b	7.2 to 10
50 to 55	12a	10 to 12.8
55 to 60	12b	12.8 to 15.6
60 to 65	13a	15.6 to 18.3
65 to 70	13b	18.3 to 21.1

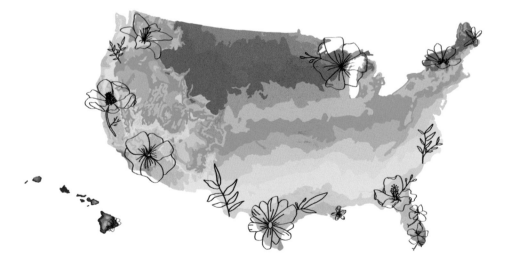

sunlight, starting out with containers will allow you to move the containers around your yard or patio as you search for those prime sun spots.

* If you do plan on digging in your yard in the United States, you can call 811 to check with utilities in your area to be sure you don't dig and accidentally disturb any underground utility lines.

When you're ready to lay out the borders of your growing space, you don't have to think in terms of costly fences and elaborate borders. Look around your yard and put to use any branches or large rocks you may already have lying around. If you'll be growing mint (page 120) or other fast-spreading plants, you can slow their spread by planting a rock border around them, though in year two your mint plant will probably find a way to spread anywhere and everywhere. If this is a concern, you can always relegate these plants to their own pot or container.

Once you have mapped out a good spot for your garden and have a general idea of what you'd like to plant, it's a good idea to jot down some notes on how much space each plant will need. Crowding too many plants in a small area will keep them from having the space they need to stretch out and thrive. "Companion planting," such as planting basil and parsley around your tomato plants, will create a harmonious aroma, and many gardeners swear by the combination. As the tomatoes grow tall in the late summer sun, they shade the basil and parsley and keep them from getting too hot. The aroma from the basil is thought to keep aphids and other pests away, though scientific evidence is scant on this topic. But even with companion planting, what's most important is to give the plants their proper space. Tomatoes, for example, require 2 to 3 feet of space around each plant for air circulation and proper root development. If you're starting from seed or buying starters from your local garden center, keep in mind the spatial needs of different

GARDEN VERMOUTH

2 lemons

2 (750-ml) bottles dry white wine

6 ounces rich simple syrup
(2 parts sugar to 1 part water)

½ cup violet flowers

⅓ cup tomato leaves, chopped

3 large sprigs of mint

3 sprigs of thyme

3 sprigs of parsley, chopped

3 sprigs of lemon balm

2 sprigs of lavender

1 sprig of rosemary

1 sprig of fresh wormwood
(the key ingredient and bitter element
of the oldest vermouths),
or 1 teaspoon dried

10 dandelion flowers

6 to 8 honeysuckle blossoms,
if available

4 basil leaves, torn

1 dried bay leaf,
or 2 fresh bay leaves, torn

Peel the lemons, removing as much pith as possible. Place the peels in a low (150°F) oven or in a dehydrator for a half hour to dry (reserve the lemons to use in a salad dressing or whiskey sour). When dry, transfer the peels to a sealable container, add the remaining ingredients, and shake well to combine. Store in the refrigerator and let the ingredients infuse for 3 days, shaking occasionally. After 3 days, strain out the botanicals and bottle your vermouth in a sealable bottle. It will stay fresh in the refrigerator for 6 to 8 weeks, but will be best for the first 3 weeks.

varieties by noting the directions on the seed packet or consulting with the nursery.

So, once you've planned and planted your garden, how do you begin putting those ingredients to work? One of my favorite things to do with early-summer garden bounty, when the herbs are vibrant and the tomatoes have yet to mature and ripen, is to make a Garden Vermouth using small clippings of herbs and tomato leaves.

This Garden Vermouth is a perfect addition to any of the French and Italian "sidewalk sips" so frequently drunk in cafés and court-yards all over southern Europe. A little vermouth here, some bit-ter aperitif like Campari, Aperol, or their gentian-forward French counterparts, Salers, Suze, or Bonal, a touch of soda or sparkling wine, and a little piece of herb or a slice of lemon for garnish is all you need. If spritzing is your thing, simply add sparkling wine to your Garden Vermouth, garnish with some herbs, and sip the afternoon away.

THE SHIFTING SEASONS

One important thing to keep in mind as you consider how to use your garden bounty is planning for the confluence of seasons. This is especially valuable with herbs, since many herbs are so hardy they can last all through the fall and winter (here's looking at you rosemary, sage, and thyme), depending on your growing zone. Basil is an herb that will surprise you with how long it will last into the fall. As your summer basils begin to go to seed, you can plant other basils in spots in your garden where you know they'll get enough sun as summer fades into fall. You can try using long-term weather forecasts or putting your trust in the Farmer's Almanac to try and predict the timing of the shifting of seasons in any given year. But those can be unreliable models (no offense to the Almanac, an indispensable tool for the home gardener). The best way to predict the shifts in season is to go by all the data compiled in previous years. Obtaining the previous average temperatures and fluctuations in daylight and rainfall is the best way to predict what will happen down the road, as even 10-day weather forecasts are notoriously inaccurate. Shifts in seasons can make it a little difficult for professionals in the beverage industry who use fresh ingredients to keep up with what they're making and what's coming next. And I've found that there aren't actually four distinct seasons; there are instead waves that ripple back and forth, offering up short-lived windows where trees flower, roots become too tough to use, and some ingredients are only perfect for a short time. What follows is an "ingredient index" of sorts to give you plenty of ideas to work with and plan out your drinking calendar, trying to take into account as many growing zones as possible.

My biggest takeaway in compiling and looking over this complete list, which you may have plenty to add to if you live in a completely different region, is that different seasons are harmonious with each other, and there are plenty of drink ideas lying in the space between seasons. For instance, orchard fruits like apple and pear, along with late summer fruits like figs, seem to go quite well with the more savory herbs like thyme, rosemary, and sage. This can help guide you along the way to creating amazing drinks.

THE BITTER TRUTH

Vermouth. Absinthe. Gentian. Foreign words conjuring vibrant, possibly mysterious characters who drink in close-quartered cafés on side streets in New Orleans, maybe Paris. But like characters in an old book suddenly revived and blown up on the big screen, these formerly dusty old counterparts are back as leading players in the new golden age of the cocktail. One of the main stars of the show in this cocktail revival of the last decade has undoubtedly been the Negroni (the Oscar for Best Supporting Role goes to the Aperol Spritz). One of Italy's main contributions to the cocktail canon, the Negroni is an equal-parts mixture of gin, sweet vermouth, and Campari, one of those simple three-ingredient drinks that begs to be a template for using all the wild, slightly bitter, mildly sweet, herbaceous liqueurs and spirits currently filling the shelves of bottle shops. The key to these flavorful spirits and liqueurs lies in the natural world: while their base, whether it's wine, a neutral grain spirit, or grappa, will have an effect on how the final product tastes, it's the botanicals growing on farms, in gardens, and in the wild that make these elixirs what they are: timeless.

In drinking as in gardening, it's best to begin simply. What I appreciate about the drinking traditions of France and Italy is that there is a clear starting point to the evening: the *apéritif* in France or, as it's known in Italy, the *aperitivo*. This can be as simple as having a small glass of vermouth and a few olives, or a Negroni with an orange slice and a piece of cheese. In France it could be a small glass of cassis with dry white wine, or anise-flavored pastis on the rocks with some mint cordial. It's not about filling time and hunger

A SEASONAL CALENDAR OF
INGREDIENTS

PRE-SPRING

Pine
Sage
Rosemary
Noble rot rose hips
Cedar
Juniper
Hazelnuts
Pomegranate
Citrus
Lemongrass

SPRING

Peas
Parsley
Strawberries
Violets
Turnips
Carrots
Young mints
Sassafras
Mulberry
Lemon balm

EARLY SPRING

Fennel
Redbud
Dandelion
Rhubarb
Greens
Root shoots of wild carrot,
sassafras, wild fennel
Beets
Lemon thyme
Sorrel

LATE SPRING/ EARLY SUMMER

Strawberries
Blueberries
Mints
Lavender
Lemon balm
Young basils
Woodruff
Flowering thyme
Bean blossoms
Melon blossoms
Honeysuckle

MIDSUMMER

Black raspberries
Elderflower
Peaches
Blackberries
Lavender
Flowering basils
Sages
Squash blossom
Walnuts
Green Peppers

LATE SUMMER

Tomatoes
Peaches
Peppers
Melons
Dill
Watermelon
Roses/zinnias
Goldenrod
Shiso
Paw paw
Passionfruit
Fig leaves
Sumac
Lilac
Nasturtium
Prickly pear

EARLY FALL

Apples
Pears
Figs
Pumpkin
Birch
Persimmon
Black walnut

FALL

Thyme
Nocino
Hickory
Maple
Cranberry
Coffee
Kale garnish
Bay laurel

CHRISTMAS/ HOLIDAY

Pine
Douglas fir
Chartreuse
Marshmallow
Génépy
Chocolate
Hazelnuts

WINTER

Hazelnuts
Citrus
Cranberry
Winter savory
Asian pear
Bay laurel

GARDENER'S
SPRITZ

1½ ounces Cocchi Americano
(a moscato-based Italian vermouth)
¾ ounce fresh-squeezed grapefruit juice
½ ounce Aperol
Soda water (preferably Topo Chico)
1 sprig of wormwood (pictured) or rosemary, for garnish
Grapefruit peel, for garnish

In a tall glass filled with ice, combine the
Cocchi Americano, grapefruit juice, and Aperol.
Stir ingredients to incorporate and top with soda
water. Garnish with rosemary and a piece of
grapefruit peel.

with a snack before dinner; it's a reset from the worries and work of the day to the joys of dinner; a chance to wind down and spend time with friends and loved ones. I mention these light and low-alcohol drinks with bold flavors for two reasons: they're a great way to start making drinks at home without breaking the bank by splurging on an entire back-bar setup, and they are the perfect end to a day spent working in the dirt outside as you prepare and plan your garden. These drinks don't require tools. Pour a little vermouth here, add a touch of soda there, toss in some basil leaves, swirl it around, and voila, you have a light and complex beverage to begin your evening. Many of these drinks use the "build in glass" method, or as I like to abbreviate it, B-I-G. This tossed-off, laid-back European approach to light and often fizzy cocktails is a refreshing reward for the dirt-digging work of a day in the garden. Try this Gardener's Spritz—ideally using Topo Chico sparkling water from Mexico, which has a luscious salinity that helps to tame the bitter and sweet flavors of the Cocchi and Aperol.

The French gentian liqueurs are fascinating spirits because there aren't many liqueurs with these vibrant spring-like flavors in other cultures. Gentian root is one of the most essential botanicals in the world of cocktails. Chances are, if you've been in a bar, you've been around gentian-based products, as gentian is one of the key bittering agents in Angostura bitters, Campari, Fernet Branca, and a peculiarly delicious old-school American soda known as Moxie. It was also an important additive to early beer recipes, until hops became more prevalent. Gentian is native to the Swiss Alps, where the plants thrive in the tall mountains, growing up to four feet tall. In early fall the root is dug up and dried and used in all manner of bitter applications all over the world. France is notable because it gives us the most pure expression of gentian in liquid form. If you want to know what the essence of gentian root smells like, just take in the aroma of Salers (my favorite) or Suze. These liqueurs evoke the bitter joys of those early spring days in the garden so well, and they make for a perfect mixer to go along with many of the botanicals popping up in the garden, wanted or unwanted. Which brings us to our beautiful, honey-scented friend on the cover, the almighty dandelion, whose flowers have an affinity for gentian root and whose root can be used in place of the bitter Swede. These springtime "weeds" are just one of the many treasures you can forage from the natural world while waiting for your garden to come into full bloom.

CHAPTER

2

THE
WORLD IS
YOUR
GARDEN

*Welcome to
the Terroir Dome*

The eye-opening moment for me as a forager (though at the time I was merely a man nearly lost in the woods) came on June 24, St. John's Day, which is an annual public holiday in Italy, specifically in the cities of Florence, Turin, and Genoa. I was on the hunt for green walnuts to make Nocino, a traditional Italian liqueur often drunk as a digestif to settle the stomach after a big meal. The tradition of making Nocino from these unripened black walnuts goes back thousands of years to the Picts (from the Latin *picti*, which means "painted") in Britain, so named by the Romans due to the fact that they would paint their skin blue. In short, these were some *trippy* folks, who believed that drinking this spiced walnut concoction would allow them to converse with goblins, elves, gods and goddesses. Did I mention they painted themselves *blue*? On the night of June 23 and into the morning of June 24, the Picts would send their most agile women up into the walnut trees barefoot to collect the precious nuts and drop them onto the ground, to become "impregnated" by the magic of the early morning dew. After having a fire and dancing and singing songs all night, our totally badass Pictian friends would then quarter the dew-kissed walnuts and plunge them into alcohol to begin the maceration process. After a few months, with spices and sugar added along the way, the Nocino would be ready to drink by the first slight chill in the night air.

When the Roman Empire made Christianity the official religion in 313 AD, many of these old traditions morphed to reflect traditions of the Bible. St. John's birth was celebrated on June 24, so the Nocino tradition blended into the significance of that day, even though it was based on a much older ritual that was not exactly *Italian.* I learned all of this when I was researching uses for black walnuts at Husk, knowing that they grew on trees all over Middle Tennessee. It struck a chord with me that I was supposed to be gathering walnuts for Nocino on a certain day in order to begin a process where the liqueur would be ready to drink by fall, which happens to be a perfect time to be drinking Nocino. So I set out to find some walnuts and followed some important foraging guidelines that I'd like to share:

* I went hiking on a long public park trail that took me deep into the woods where I was sure no pesticides had been sprayed.

* Though it was summer in Tennessee and it was going to be hot, I wore pants and long sleeves for protection from bugs and any rough vegetation I would encounter. I also lathered myself up with some natural bug spray to help keep the ticks away. If you're going to be out in the elements, be prepared for all nature can throw your way.

* I carried a pocket knife, to cut tree limbs, or any plant debris that may get in the way.

* I had studied the identification of walnuts and cross-checked their features against those of potentially poisonous look-alikes. Luckily, walnuts are so aromatic they nearly bowl you over with their scent, making them easy to identify. After an hour of gathering them, I had a slight headache from the intensity of the aroma. It's no wonder that it nearly drove pagans mad with passion!

* I wore gloves to pick, and more importantly, to process the walnuts. They can stain your skin like a month-long temporary tattoo.

* I took along some water and went with a buddy. Depending on how far you will be venturing, it's important to take a map to keep track of where you are, and it's always safer with a friend.

When I mentioned it was an eye-opening experience, it wasn't just the walnuts and their powerful aroma that blew me away. It was *everything else* I saw along the way. Elderflower with its summery peach perfume, small sassafras saplings ready to be dug and used for tea or root beer, wild blackberries providing a nice snack through the thorns, wild carrot (Queen Anne's lace) blooming everywhere, and sumac splashing early-summer bright red color all around me. Even wild pink roses were starting to bloom. So don't worry if your garden is not producing as much as you'd like, or if you feel like you don't have enough growing space for your beverage needs. There is a whole world of ingredients out there waiting for you. But before we get to more of these ingredients in depth, here is my Nocino recipe—and don't forget the gloves!

THE DEMONIZATION OF THE DANDELION

When Kate and I sold the first house we bought, complete with the 360-degree garden I had worked so hard on over the years and learned so much from, it was difficult to imagine starting a new garden from scratch. But my appreciation for all the plants growing *outside* the garden served me well as I began to plan another one five miles north of our first house. When spring began sprouting, I kept a close eye on where the sunlight was falling in my backyard. One day before beginning to dig, I noticed that a wild botanical, the Japanese herb perilla, or shiso, a lovely basil-like herb I had searched high and low for in years past, was spreading all over my backyard. I chalked it up to some forager's karma or good gardening mojo, but the truth turned out to be that the old inhabitants of my house had a large pond in the backyard where they raised Koi fish, and they also grew some traditional Japanese herbs. Now each summer I have shiso bordering an entire section of my garden, and instead of searching for it, I only have to cut it back now and then to keep it from taking over. As time goes on, an inquisitive mind can be the gardener's best friend. The more plants you are able to identify with certainty, the less you'll see things in your yard or your neighborhood as black and white, good and bad. Many

NOCINO

11 green walnuts, quartered
(in keeping with tradition,
go for an odd number of walnuts)

2 quarts pure grain alcohol

2 quarts water

4 quarts sugar

4 cardamom pods, cracked

4 cinnamon sticks,
crushed with the back of a skillet
on a towel on a firm countertop

3 star anise pods

2 tablespoons whole cloves

Zest of 2 lemons

IN LATE JUNE:

Place the walnuts in a 64-ounce Mason jar and fill the jar with grain alcohol, leaving an inch of space at the top. Let the walnuts infuse for 2 months in a cool, dry area at room temperature, shaking the jar once a week.

AFTER 2 MONTHS:

In a large pot, combine the water, sugar, cardamom, cinnamon sticks, star anise, and cloves and bring to a medium simmer. Simmer for 20 minutes, then remove from the heat and place in the refrigerator to infuse overnight.

continued →

THE NEXT DAY:

Strain the spiced syrup and discard the whole spices. Add the lemon zest to the strained syrup. Wearing gloves, strain the walnut infusion and discard the walnuts. Add the spiced syrup and lemon zest to the walnut infusion and set aside in a cool, dark place for 1 month to let the flavors meld and rest together.

WHEN READY TO DRINK:

Strain out the lemon zest and bottle the nocino. You now have one of the oldest and most delicious liqueurs known to humans! Paint yourself blue and drink some by a large fire. Or try my Manhattan variation (page 44), which also happens to go great with a fire.

of the "weeds" we look to get rid of should actually be classified as herbs, since an herb can be defined as a plant that "has use or benefit."

Take for instance the extremely common broadleaf plantain, a spinach-like green that sprouts up in open spaces everywhere and may just be hanging out all over your yard come May and June. Not only can it be cooked and eaten like spinach, it also has incredible healing properties when chewed and applied to a bee sting or other bug bite. If you live in the Northern or Central United States, there's a magical wild cousin of the chamomile herb with an unforgettably tropical aroma known as "pineapple weed" that grows everywhere. While in Charleston, South Carolina, one spring, I noticed many of the alleyways smelled like perfume only to realize it was the wisteria vine, another wildflower perfect for infusing into cordials and liqueurs, as well as for its traditional use, decorating birthday cakes. Another ingredient that grows all over the United States but is rarely used—which is puzzling, as it is so common in distant, exotic cuisines—is sumac. While poisonous sumac has white fruits, this variety is extremely rare to find in the wilds of America. The more common varieties you'll begin to see if you keep your eye out for them are staghorn sumac, winged sumac, and smooth sumac, with its beautiful red berries. The fruit can be dried and used as a spice, or it can be made into a delicious beverage by infusing the ripe late-summer sumac berries into a pitcher of cold water for half an hour, then straining them out and drinking the infusion with a cordial of your choice or a bit of sugar. The taste and color are akin to pink lemonade.

And of course, when it comes time to clear some space for a garden, or to clear out the early spring newcomers to make space for more established botanicals like lemon balm, borage, and basil, dandelion is one of the first maligned "weeds" to go. The demonization of the dandelion is such that it is the face (literally, it's on

PICTS AND ME ROLLIN'

1 ounce good rye whiskey
(like Pikesville)

1 ounce Laird's Apple Brandy

1 ounce Nocino (page 39)

¼ ounce Carpano Antica

1 dash Angostura bitters

Very tiny pinch of Maldon sea salt

Orange twist, for garnish

Combine all the ingredients except the lemon in a
mixing glass. Add plenty of ice and stir until well
chilled. Strain into a rocks glass over a few large
ice cubes and garnish with an orange twist.

DANDELION
FLOWER CORDIAL

3 quarts water

4 quarts sugar

2 quarts dandelion flowers (divided),
pinched from their stems,
washed thoroughly in cold water,
and set aside to dry for a few hours

1/3 cup orange blossom honey
or other light honey
(no dark wildflower honey here;
the flavor is too powerful)

Zest of 2 lemons

Bring the water to a boil, lower the heat to a medium simmer, and add the sugar and 1 quart of the dandelion flowers. Simmer for 20 minutes, then promptly remove from the heat. Stir in the honey and let the syrup cool. After it has cooled, cover the syrup and refrigerate overnight. Add the remaining quart of dandelion flowers the following day, along with the lemon zest, and let the syrup infuse for another 2 days in the refrigerator. Over the course of those 2 days, taste the cordial as it infuses and add more fresh dandelions to increase the flavor if you like. Just remember to pinch them off the stems and wash them well under cold water.

the bottle of a certain weed killer) of all that has come to invade your own personal Augusta, your manicured felt table of perfection known as the *lawn*. But I would urge you to experiment with this wild botanical growing all around us. If an herb is defined as "a plant of use," the dandelion would certainly qualify. Used in such vaunted liqueurs as Yellow Chartreuse (page 190) and bittersweet Salers and Suze, it has digestive and diuretic benefits and, according to Susun Weed, author of *Healing Wise* and a champion of the dandelion, it can boost the immune system as well as heart and liver function. Before picking dandelions, however, you must be certain that no pesticides have been sprayed on them, which takes a healthy botanical and turns it into a toxic one. Use the leaves in springtime salads, as they provide a nice bitter balance to the juicy, vibrant flavors of good fresh lettuce. And if you don't want to order Swiss gentian online for making bitters and cordials, digging up the dandelion root, washing it and drying it for a few days, and chopping it up and storing in a sealed container away from sunlight will provide you with a fresh, local bittering agent to use in all of your Garden-to-Glass applications. But the flower itself holds so much beautiful honeyed flavor, it would be a crime not to use it while you wait for your other plants to develop! When picking the flowers, simply pinch them from their stems to ensure continued production.

My goal with this cordial is to simulate what dandelion honey would taste like, with the dandelion flavor certainly shining through. The honey and the lemon zest only serve to bring out those respective flavors of the flower itself. I'd encourage anyone making cordials to use this as a guide: When showcasing a particular ingredient, utilize the subtle tasting notes of that ingredient to round out the flavors of your cordial. For example, lemon balm and lemon verbena are obvious choices to use with lemon, and since lemon balm and some varieties of thyme share a flavor affinity, you can add a small piece of thyme to a lemon-herb cordial to add complexity and depth and bring out the herbal flavor in cocktails. This is something we'll cover in depth in Chapter 9, "Cordials and the Art of Finishing."

Another essential wild botanical for use in cocktails and beverages is Japanese honeysuckle, which grows abundantly all over the United States in all but seven states. In the house where I dug my first large-scale garden, I used to joke that nature was looking down on me and laughing as I waited for herbs, flowers, and vegetables to come to life. I had rushes of honeysuckle growing all over the backyard that seemed to beckon my attention, saying, "Hey! Over here! There's plenty of us to go around!" The smell would drift across the yard like a lazy fly in early summer, providing me some solace through my early trial-and-error days in the garden. Honeysuckle and other fragrant spring and summer flowers have many uses but are particularly well suited for infusion into spirits, liqueurs, and cordials, as well as to use as garnishes. Garnishes are often a forgotten cost in the creation of a cocktail, and while edible flowers are available from plenty of purveyors, it can be difficult to obtain flowers with their potent aromas still intact. When picked fresh, the honeysuckle flower retains its unmistakable aroma and adds a floral complexity to any drink simply by sitting on top of it. It can also be a memorable flower for so many people, as it's often the first "taste" any of us ever had of the wild, natural world. I've found that a lot of people connect with it, and have fond stories of tasting that first drop of nectar when they were kids. It's hard to put a price on that type of sensory connection a guest can have with one drink. To keep honeysuckle fresh for garnish at the peak of its season, follow these guidelines:

* Be sure to harvest in an area that has not been sprayed with pesticides.

* Try to harvest honeysuckle in mid-morning before the temperature is too hot outside.

HONEYSUCKLE LIQUEUR

2 quarts sugar

1 quart water

1 quart lightly packed honeysuckle blossoms,
washed under cold water and patted dry

2 cups Cathead Honeysuckle Vodka

Zest and juice of 2 lemons

½ cup fresh chamomile flowers,
or ¼ cup dried chamomile

2 drops orange blossom water

Cook the sugar and water over low heat to dissolve
the sugar, then promptly remove from the heat. Add
the honeysuckle, vodka, lemon zest and juice, chamomile, and orange blossom water. Refrigerate for 3
days to allow the flavors to infuse, then strain out
the solids, and bottle. The liqueur will keep in the
refrigerator for months. To make this a cordial, take
out the vodka, but note that the cordial will only keep
for around a month in the refrigerator.

* Using garden shears or a good sharp pocket knife, cut off honeysuckle vines in 12- to 18-inch lengths, plunging the branches into 4 to 6 inches of ice water as soon after cutting as you can. Leave the flowers on the vines. Honeysuckle is classified as invasive, so don't worry, it'll grow back with aplomb.

* Harvesting vines with blossoms that haven't fully opened yet can give you the opportunity to use the blossoms right after they've bloomed.

* If you pass by your favored honeysuckle spot and notice that the blooms are gone, wait until a good rain has fallen in the area, then go back and see if the blooms have returned. With periodic heavy rain, honeysuckle can hang around all summer and deep into fall.

Making your own honeysuckle liqueur is very easy, and I use a honeysuckle vodka to add another layer of that delicate floral flavor. This honeysuckle vodka from Cathead Distillery in Mississippi is available in 16 states as of this printing, but if you can't find it where you live, see if your local liquor store can order it. One thing you may be surprised at is how much honeysuckle it takes for the flavor to shine through.

While we're on the topic of wildflowers tailor-made for drinks, let's look at one of the most misunderstood and mysteriously flavored wildflowers: elderflower, or as it's known to many botanists, flowering elderberry. At some point over the last few years, St. Germain, the elderflower liqueur from France, has become so widely used by bartenders it has wound up with the rather unfortunate title of "bartender's ketchup." While that may not be particularly inspiring from a "who's thirsty" perspective, I have seen it used with almost every spirit, and that is to be respected. I've personally used it in drinks that are simple, complicated, even strange, yet its most likely application is in drinks meant to please even the stingiest of weekend warriors. In short, it's a crowd-pleaser, and it has an alchemical singularity that I would best describe as honeyed-grapefruit-peel-meets-proprietary-French-perfume,with a dash of cinnamon. But after spending a *lot* of time over the past six years searching for, harvesting, and infusing actual fresh elder-flower, I can confirm one thing that St. Germain does *not* taste like: elderflower. I'm not trying to knock it at all; it is a delicious liqueur that's featured on cocktail menus around the world. But the actual essence of real elderflower is a flavor so dainty and hard to pin down, like a tiny little fairy that darts through the forest, over the meadows, and just out of reach, that one must actually seek it out, sprinkling the blossoms over a fruit salad or dunking them into an infusion, to capture their true flavor.

One of the keys to finding elderflower is being able to identify it. The leaves are slightly toothed, with a mild serrated edge to them, and the flowers burst forth from light green stems holding jangly florets. The flowers have five petals, which can help distinguish elderflower from other toxic or poisonous lookalikes such as cow-bane, pokeweed, and cow parsley. The aroma is best described with the hopelessly nonspecific characterization, "creamy." There is an unmistakably summery scent to it, and if you find enough of it, you can be relatively choosy and pick only the most fragrant blossoms, foregoing any that have been overly scorched by the sun, befallen by a light brown color around the blossoms. The sea-son is relatively short, and if you want to use both elderflower *and* elderberry from the same foraging spot, you'll have to leave some flowers to mature into berries in the early fall. Elderflower needs to be lightly washed in cold water and infused almost immediately, as it will lose its lovely aroma over the course of 24 to 48 hours. And be sure to pick your elderflower away from any roadsides, espe-cially busy roads where pollution is plentiful. It's best to travel with a jug of cold water that you can safely dunk the stems into upon

ELDERFLOWER CORDIAL

4 quarts sugar

2 quarts water

I tablespoon citric acid

10 large elderflower heads,
trimmed with no stem attached to the umbels,
shaken lightly to release any bugs
and rinsed (not drenched)
in lightly running cold water

I peach, not quite ripened with firm flesh, diced

Zest of I grapefruit

Zest of I lemon

⅓ cup orange blossom honey
or other light honey

2 tablespoons Lindera Farms Elderflower Vinegar,
or I squeeze of lemon juice

Combine the sugar, water, and citric acid in a pot over low heat and cook, stirring until the sugar is dissolved. Transfer the syrup to a clean container and place in the refrigerator to cool completely. (Using the "cold process method" helps to maintain the freshness of the elderflower and retain that summery, creamy aroma that is its signature.) When the syrup is cool, add the elderflowers, peach, citrus zest, honey, and vinegar and return to the refrigerator to infuse for 3 to 4 days, adding more elderflower as needed, or as you find more! It's hard to have *too* much elderflower in this cordial. The flavor of fresh elderflower is exquisite, so taste your cordial every day and add more elderflower as you see fit. When ready to drink, strain the liquid without agitating the ingredients to avoid clouding your cordial. Store in the refrigerator and use within 3 weeks.

picking it in order to keep it as fresh as possible in transit. When you get home, or arrive at the kitchen of your restaurant or bar, making Elderflower Cordial should be your first priority.

Another delicious application for elderflower is naturally sparkling Elderflower Champagne, which uses the naturally occurring yeasts in the elderflower to bolster fermentation. Since wild yeasts are abundant on berries, and mulberries, with their grape-soda flavor-bomb sweetness, and usually appear at the same time as elderflower, we'll combine the two wild-yeast-harboring ingredients into one refreshing summer beverage. If mulberries (which, unlike blackberries and raspberries, actually grow on trees) are difficult to find in your area, you'll need a packet of champagne yeast from your local brewing store, and some blackberries or blueberries from the market. Since the flavor of elderflower is so elusive and mild, the mulberries, blackberries, or blueberries are used for their yeasts as well as to give tannin, structure, color, and a light fruity taste to the final fizzy product.

FLAVOR DOES GROW ON TREES

Though mulberry is an often forgotten summer berry, it grows in abundance on trees throughout the United States, predominantly in growing zones 4 to 8, which covers *most* of the United States. Other wild berries, from the elusive wild strawberries to blueberries to the more common wild blackberries and black raspberries, are a welcome sight on a long hike and give you plenty of options beyond what you can do with berries from the store. Just as you can grow herbs to use them in different stages of their growth, like growing dill for its flowers or to use the stems for straws, finding wild berries allows you to use them at different stages of maturity. Unripened berries, for example, have a lot of acid and can give a bright "tang" to any cocktail or nonalcoholic beverage. Try the sherry cobbler recipe (one of the original "fancy" cocktails), where

MULBERRY
ELDERFLOWER
CHAMPAGNE

2 gallons warm water

1 quart sugar

Zest and juice of 4 organic lemons

¼ cup Lindera Farms Chamomile Vinegar,
or champagne vinegar

10 large elderflower heads

2 cups wild mulberries,
or blueberries or blackberries

Packet (5 grams) of champagne yeast,
if needed

Place the warm water in a sterilized pot, crock, or fermentation vessel and stir in the sugar. Add the zest of the lemons, then squeeze them to release all the lemon juice into the container. Add the juiced lemon hulls to the mixture. Next add the vinegar, elderflower heads, and mulberries and stir to incorporate. Cover tightly with a clean cloth and leave in a cool place for a few days, checking for any bubbling or fermentation action from time to time. You will want to see some magic happening in the form of occasional bubbling and a little white foam forming on top. If after 3 days you don't see any action, add some champagne yeast and let it sit for another day or two. Strain the mixture into another sterilized vessel, but do not press down on the solids as you strain. (This is known as a gravity strain, which helps maintain a more consistent color and won't release too much tannin.) Transfer the liquid to bottles with good, strong swivel tops, cap them, and store in a cool, dark place for 3 to 5 more days, releasing a little of the pressure in the bottles every few days. After a week of this secondary fermentation, store the bottles in the refrigerator to halt fermentation, and send a group text to your friends: "Who wants fizzy summer in a glass?"

you shake in unripened berries to brighten up the savory flavors of the sherry.

To be able to identify mulberries, as well as all the other ingredients in this book, it will serve you well to have a guidebook or two. I recommend *Stalking the Healthful Herbs* by Euell Gibbons, as well as Lee Peterson's *Field Guide to Edible Wild Plants*. But one of my favorites for my own region is Chris Bennett's *Foraging the Southeast*, which has photo identification and also includes some general recipe ideas that will have you baking, blanching, and imbibing. I was fortunate to take some long walks with Chris's guidance a few years back in Nashville, along with chef Brian Baxter. Chris is wise beyond his years and very passionate about food and drink—not to mention a talented cheesemaker, with great taste in vinyl records. I drank some ice cold absinthe with Chris and discussed foraging and summertime, as well as the joys and dangers of venturing into the wild for ingredients.

> **MW:** Aside from your book, which is a great resource for those of us living in the Southeast, are there other fundamental books that you could recommend about foraging?

> **CHRIS BENNET AKA FORAGERMAN** (used from here on out): Yes, any book by Samuel Thayer. His first two books, *The Forager's Harvest* and *Nature's Garden*, are essential. Also, any of the regional foraging guides put out by Timber Press are great resources. There's a lot of overlap in wild plants between the Midwest, Northeast, and Southeast. It can also help to have a guide to wildflowers and trees.

> **MW:** That's good insight. Seems like that would help broaden one's identification powers. You've written about the importance of identifying plants and cross-checking them with

WILD BERRY SHERRY COBBLER

1 teaspoon superfine sugar

2 lemon peels,
with as little pith as possible

4 unripened mulberries,
black raspberries, or blackberries,
plus more for garnish

3 ounces Amontillado,
Manzanilla, or Fino Sherry

1 sprig of mint, for garnish

In a shaker tin, lightly muddle the sugar, lemon peels, and berries, then add the sherry and stir a little to incorporate. Add some crushed ice and a few cubes to your shaker and shake until well chilled and frosty. Double strain over crushed ice, garnish with more berries and a large sprig of mint, and serve with a compostable straw. Legend has it that the Sherry Cobbler was the drink that helped popularize the straw—just take care not to drink it all in 30 seconds.

poisonous lookalikes. What are some of the dangers of foraging in general?

FORAGERMAN: Always be 100% sure of the plant you are eating before you eat it. You can easily poison yourself or other people. Being able to correctly identify plants is paramount. There's also all the dangers of being outdoors. Like poison ivy, wild animals, ticks, etc.

MW: Do you have a favorite plant to use in beverage form? If so, what application or methods do you use?

FORAGERMAN: That's a tough one! I would say in the summertime, my favorite is sumac. There are several types of edible sumac that grow in the Southeast. I love taking the fresh "berries," and rubbing the ascorbic acid off while submerged in cold water. It produces a pinkish colored water that is sour and tart. From there the sky is the limit. When thinking of how to use something I always think of the flavor profile. Vodka definitely comes to mind when using sumac. Also, I love making shrubs with sumac!

MW: Ethics and foraging are two things that go hand in hand in your work as a writer and gatherer. What can people do to be smarter about how they forage?

FORAGERMAN: Sustainability has always been an integral part of foraging. You never want to take everything from a particular spot, with a few exceptions. One easy way of foraging sustainably, is by clipping instead of stripping a plant of its leaves. By clipping, you will allow the plant to regrow. If you just strip the leaves it will soon die.

MW: Why can I never find pineapple weed, especially now that I've got a tiki bar?

FORAGERMAN: (laughs) I think it's because it doesn't grow very far south. I've seen it as far south as Maryland, but even then it was spotty. I would be curious to see if it's something you can grow from seed.

We'll talk more in later chapters about other wild ingredients that can be used for garnishes and fresh cordials. There is no shortage of plants to seek out while you wait for your herb starters to mature or your burgeoning mint and basil patches to become full on "garnish gardens." Sometimes all it takes is a good long walk to find all the garnish you need, or to spark a new idea for a drink you hadn't thought of before. With a little knowledge and an attentive eye for detail, you can expand your Garden to Glass ingredient library and use plants that are so fresh, they are literally thriving all around you. All it takes is being resourceful, with an emphasis on the *source*. And one of the best times to have your antennae up is when those first few daffodil bulbs begin to sprout and the neighborhood looks like an old TV set changing from black and white to color, during the can't-come-too-soon glory of spring. In the springtime months when I was finishing this book, I learned an intense lesson about the cycle of life, love, the value of companionship, and how a simple garden interacts with the entire universe around it.

CHAPTER

3

CYCLES
OF LIFE

&

LOSS

with the
Barefoot Farmer

pring was in full swing in Middle Tennessee, and I had been planning a trip about an hour north from Nashville up to Red Boiling Springs to see gardening and biodynamic farming legend Jeff Poppen, aka the Barefoot Farmer. If there is such a thing as a rock star farmer in our region, he was the *guy*. He even had his own band and organized music festivals on his farm during the summer and winter solstices. While I was managing the bar at Husk, deliveries of his produce into our walk-in were very special occasions. Baskets upon baskets would flow out of his truck and into the restaurant. The match of creativity would be immediately struck, as chefs would begin to ponder how best to capture these biodynamically grown little masterpieces such as his famous garlic and sweet potatoes. There aren't many farmers who can walk barefoot into a fine dining restaurant, but here was one who could and would and did it with humor, depth, knowledge, and compassion. "We can save the world by growing things in the ground," he would say, which can be dismissed as something said between tokes while sitting on a blanket at a music festival, but coming from Barefoot, sounded like something we all needed to get on board with. He once hung out in the bar at Husk and enjoyed a meal with some of his best friends, before walking down the hill to see the Marshall Tucker Band play into the night. While at the bar, talk turned to the 160-year-old oak tree that towered like a sky-scraper above Rutledge Hill overlooking downtown Nashville. The tree was clearly not doing well, the roots possibly disturbed by all the dynamite that was being used to dig out a new parking garage just a few blocks down the hill. Many in the neighborhood worried it would have to be cut down. Barefoot was clearly moved by the situation. Later that night at closing time, as I dragged the bar mats outside for their nightly spray down, I glanced over at the tree to see Barefoot and his friends singing to the tree and gathering around to hug its mammoth trunk. That image stuck with me ever since and I knew I had to reconnect with him for this book.

It was shaping up as one of the last things I needed to get done. Then one of the saddest days of my life happened.

My best friend of nearly eight years, a Blue merle Great Dane we named Merle (both for his color and in honor of Merle Haggard), died in my arms on the couch—not my couch, it had been "his" couch for a long time. Like so many Great Danes, Merle had digestive problems throughout his life, but we had managed it the best we could with meds and a special diet, even trying kangaroo at one point. He had a big yard to make his own and forced my hand when it came time to put a small fence around my garden. If Merle was out in the garden and got startled (some Great Danes really are like Scooby Doo) he could take a few wrong steps and destroy two tomato plants in a matter of seconds. But he loved the cool ground and stinky smells in the garden and would surprise me by jumping over or "altering" any kind of fence I would put up. He loved the funky, medicinal smell of tansy, though somehow, unlike most things he was happy to ingest like tree bark and siding, he never tried to eat any.

Merle was the ultimate pal and protector. When Kate and I had kids, he was so patient and loving to them, allowing Leila and Henry to crawl all over him and lay on his belly as he sprawled out like a rug on the floor. Guests to the house were greeted to Merle's booming baritone of a bark, followed by the high-pitched squeals of excitement when he realized one of his friends was coming into his domain. He loved nothing more than to jump on the bed and be surrounded by family, taking turns to make sure his belly was sufficiently rubbed and the spot behind his ear had been scratched in five-minute intervals. I could even get Merle to talk like Chewbacca if I fake-growled at him enough. And as I sat at the desk in my house writing this book, I was treated to a few of those moments a writer can only dream of: it's cold outside and even as warm air barrels through the old vents in the floor, there's a draft from the window by the door—I'm wearing a sweater and some slippers to keep warm, but Merle is curled up next to my chair and if the draft gets too chilly, I slip my feet between his barrel chest and long neck to get the best kind of warm: dog warmth. As I would take part in this ritual with Merle he would slowly swing his head around like he was writing an *r* with the tip of his nose.

When Merle passed, I had to look around at Kate, Leila, Henry, and our cat, Boone, and remember that I was extremely blessed in this life. I was fortunate to be there in his last moments. He was looking for me and I was there. We didn't have to make a decision at a veterinary hospital, though it all happened so fast it started to feel like an out-of-body experience. It's too hard in those moments to have any epiphanies about the cycles of life. The pain of losing the family dog, your best friend, there for you no matter how bad of a day you had, in need of your attention and love no matter how good your day was as well, puts a wall of sorrow around you that you seem to constantly collide with. You can't escape it. You might lose track of it for a few moments, but you turn and it's there. You start to feel bad in those small moments where you forgot that he's actually gone. The next day was a blur. Appointments were cancelled, and we began the process of deciding what to do with Merle's 145-pound frame.

The one appointment I felt I should keep was around 40 hours from the time Merle passed: an interview with the Barefoot Farmer on his beautiful farm to talk about the basics of gardening and age-old philosophies and techniques. Family and friends encouraged me to go out and get some air on the farm. One of those, "It'll do ya good," moments. As I set out on a gorgeous spring day in April, bright sunshine and blue sky, redbuds blooming on the county line, I tried to think positively on how best to memorialize Merle. Kate and I talked about turning some of the ashes into a rock with his name on it and setting it out by the garden. As I lost cell service and got further into the country, I had laughed and cried and even forgot where I was going and why I was driving out in the middle of nowhere. What I would find were fundamental lessons about the cycles of life and death, and how nature does what it must do with death to proliferate life. As I pulled up to the farm, I noticed two rocks on the side of the house that said "Mom" and "Dad."

Jeff Poppen, aka the Barefoot Farmer, is undoubtedly a product of his intellectual, analytical father and his flower-loving, plant-talking, worldly mother. He speaks of them often and is never far from the collection of agricultural books they introduced him to during his formative years in the 1960s and '70s. His farm in Red Boiling Springs, Tennessee, is one of the only certified biodynamic farms in the Southeast. He too had experienced loss recently as his barn, containing the seed garlic he had been saving for 35 years, burned down in the fall. Luckily no people or animals were harmed, but he lost a tractor and over 100 square bales of hay and most of his farm tools. We sat down on the sunny side of his back porch with the morning just beginning to warm up, as he awaited a delivery of scrap wood to be used for the new barn, which was set to go up in the next month.

MW: What led you to a life of growing things?

BAREFOOT: Well, I grew up on a farm in Illinois, and both my parents were avid gardeners. My father was a nursery man who knew a lot about trees and shrubbery, and my mother just loved flowers. They had a big vegetable garden and fruit orchard, and they canned all of our food. We had livestock and chickens running around and that kind of stuff. So I guess, my innate love for growing things comes from my folks. Later, my father had gotten a few PhD's in Nashville in the 1940s and had always talked highly of Tennessee being pretty and friendly.

When it came time to have my own place I bought a farm down here.

How I ended up getting into growing food was that I was hungry. I was 18 living out in the woods with no electricity, cooking on a wood stove and getting our water from a spring. During the first winter we had potatoes and kale, but not much else. The next year we put a very big garden out, and it just kept growing.

MW: On the topic of starting a garden, I've heard you talk before and read things you wrote about soil tillage being so important. What advice might you have for the home gardener starting a new garden?

BAREFOOT: Well, the first thing we look at is drainage. You have to have the land *open*, so that when it rains it doesn't puddle and when it dries out it doesn't cake and get real hard. And that is all soil tilth, and the way a gardener might do it is to dig out a trench in their garden, say 18 inches wide and 10 to 12 inches deep and just put that dirt to the side. And then take a pick and a digging fork and dig out that subsoil another 10 to 12 inches down and loosen that up and leave it down there. Don't bring it to the surface. At that point you might put some sand or some lime or gravel or something in there to keep it loose, and then go to the next trench you're going to dig and push that soil over the first trench and then keep digging that deep as you go. When you're done your garden will be dug out 22 to 24 inches deep, and you're pushing the topsoil back on. Then when you put compost on and get biological activity on the surface, what you'll have is an open soil underneath so that when it rains, water goes down into the subsoil and doesn't run off the surface, and then when it dries up, water, through capillary action, will come up from that subsurface water to your plants as the soil dries out around the plant roots.

MW: What are other important fundamental factors of a garden?

BAREFOOT: Composting is real important. We also need to think about remineralizing too. A lot of the soils of the Southeast are very poor in minerals because we didn't get the glacial activity that we did up in the Midwest. Consequentially, we need to add things like wood ashes or ground-up lime or rock phosphate to remineralize and put minerals back in.

MW: Where do those minerals need to be added in the soil?

BAREFOOT: Put those on the top. Down below you don't want quite as much fertility. You can add gravel down below to help break up clay soils, mainly to help with drainage. You want your soil to have a lot of air pockets in it, not to be squished or compacted.

MW: You are a prominent biodynamic farmer and champion of that movement. At what point did biodynamic farming become important to you and why?

BAREFOOT: Back in the '60s there was a publication called the *Whole Earth Catalog,* and it had resources for a lot of different fields of interest. One of them was organic gardening. In that section there were some reviews of different books. One was *Agriculture: An Introductory Reader* by Rudolf Steiner, another was *Companion Plants and How to Use Them* by Richard Gregg and Helen Philbrook, and another one was *Weeds and What They Tell Us* by Ehrenfried Pfeiffer. My mother bought these books for my father and we had them around a lot when I was a kid. When I had my own farm, they ended up back on my lap and I started to use some of the biodynamic preparations in those books. I was told that they don't work on faith; I didn't have to *believe* in them, they actually build better soil. So we tried them and the gardens did very well. What sold us on biodynamic techniques was the keeping quality of the vegetables. Potatoes kept extremely well for us.

I was really interested in organic gardening and farming and when you're 18, you think you know everything; by the time 23 rolls around you look around and say, "Maybe there are other people who are smarter than me." So I started traveling and going to other organic farms. The ones that I went to that were biodynamic just seemed healthier and more vibrant. So, I just kept exploring that path. That's not to say that other paths of gardening and farming aren't appropriate and good too; it's just the one that I connected with.

MW: Are there biodynamic principles that a home gardener can introduce to their practice?

BAREFOOT: Yeah, so that would be simple things like opening up your topsoil and getting your drainage correct, like we talked about. And always having half of your garden be a crop that you're just going to plow in to make the soil better. So if you want to have a 2,000-square-foot garden, have 1,000 of that just be cover crops and then the next year, rotate them. Always have a compost pile and you can definitely buy compost preparations; you don't have to make them. And another thing is to always realize that your garden is a part of something bigger. If you have a garden, you don't want to be spraying chemicals on the lawn right next to it. Realize that this is an interactive thing with something larger than just your garden. You could say it's an interactive thing with the whole earth and the whole universe and just be aware that you're a small part of all of that and it's important to play that part well.

Now, you can buy what we call the "field sprays," of the cow manure or the silica in a cow horn. It's not that hard to do really; all we do is put cow manure into a cow horn and bury it or put silica into a cow horn and bury it at different times of the year, winter and summer respectively.

A garden generally needs a farm, so a gardener should have a relationship with a farmer because that's where you can get manure for your compost and maybe some hay for mulches and then farmers often times don't have time to have a garden so you can swap out some tomatoes and squash for your garden needs and start a nice partnership there. There are always ways to work together, just like how soil microorganisms are in mutual relationships, so are humans with other humans. It's good to be aware of the billions of microbes in every spoonful and really try to treat them well, because they're the ones who grow your crop.

MW: So, silica or cow manure buried in cow horns?

BAREFOOT: To *enhance* the manure. Steiner suggested that *because* a cow has horns and hooves this is why the manure is so valuable because they radiate forces back into the belly of the cow as they digest. He suggested taking the manure and putting it in horns and burying it in the winter and taking it out in spring and stirring it with water homeopathically for about an hour and then sprinkling that onto the fields.

Then to balance the earth and water energies, which that helps with, we work with the air, light, and warmth energies by taking ground-up silica, or quartz crystals, and putting them in a cow horn and burying it in the summer months, and we take a small amount of that and stir it up and sprinkle it on the plants and this helps the plants to ripen, store better, and become more nutritious. Silica works from the periphery; it's on our fingernails and hair and the periphery of our body, whereas calcium is in our bones. In an apple the silica would be on the shine of the skin and the calcium would be in the seed.

You'll find these properties of silica working with the outside light, air, and warmth helping with nutrition and you have your calcium forces working with earth and water to make humus and growth and reproduction.

MW: Fascinating stuff. You mentioned companion planting. What are some companion plants for the everyday gardener?

BAREFOOT: We talk a lot about how each plant has stuff coming out of its roots and that's going to affect neighboring plants. Plants that get along, like beans and cucumbers, have another advantage in that cucumber vines can crawl; many bush beans do not crawl. So the cucumber reaches out to the bush bean around the time that the beans have all been picked. So you can alternate beans and cucumbers and we do this every year. Tomatoes seem to like to grow near basil, and dill is nice near cucumbers, and there are some plants who don't get along. Peas and beans don't like onions and leeks and so on. Companion planting is a very interesting thing. Marigolds help keep root nematodes away from your garden. Some plants in the Umbelliferae family—particularly the parsleys, dill, and anise and things like that—attract beneficial insects when they flower, so there's a lot of reasons to have a variety of plants around working symbiotically.

MW: And plants which enjoy each other's company seem to also taste even better when eaten together, specifically things like tomatoes with basil and cucumber with dill. They're almost dispensable without each other.

BAREFOOT: I think another thing we should point out here is that this is mostly anecdotal information being passed down from gardener to gardener. This is just people sharing their experiences with each other, which I think is really invaluable. If we're talking about things that a home gardener can do, one of the best things you can do is to get together with other gardeners in your neighborhood or area and share information. You can order fertilizer in bulk, order rock dust together, take a truck out to a farm and pick up some manure for compost, things like that. You can share cuttings of plants, maybe someone has too much of something or not enough, and you can help foster a sense of community through your garden. Don't make the mistake to think you have to do everything yourself. That's a mistake that a lot of gardeners make, but sometimes you need to lean on each other a little bit.

MW: I know you're a big music guy. You have music festivals out here on your farm occasionally and you play around locally. I'm sure you've heard about music helping plants grow. Have you ever experimented with this phenomenon?

BAREFOOT: So I knew the guy who co-wrote [with Peter Tomkins] "Secret Life of Plants," Christopher Byrd. It was a hot topic of conversation in my family. My father was an intellectual and he wasn't about to believe in anything like that, plants talking to plants. But of course my mom talked to plants (laughs)! I'd have to fall somewhere in between there. I don't talk to plants, I try to listen to them a little bit though. Honestly what bothered me about that theory is that all the bands that I liked they were saying the plants *didn't* like. Like what, plants don't like the good bands like Led Zeppelin and Jimi Hendrix? But they like freaking Mozart? What?! (Laughs) I just don't know about all that; that didn't make sense to me. Later on I heard about something called "Sonic Bloom," where you played music and sprayed something on the plants to help them bloom and grow. I don't know about all that, I guess it's all up for debate. One thing I know is musicians don't really want a 9 to 5 job and neither do farmers! That could be why so many farms host music festivals.

MW: You mentioned cover crops, which can help build up your soil and increase nutrients in your garden. What are some of your favorites?

BAREFOOT: In the summertime I like to use buckwheat because it helps to mobilize calcium that's unavailable to other plants. Buckwheat can access it and when it gets plowed under it becomes accessible to the next crop. And also the legume family, which would include things like black-eyed peas or any kind of bean, and those are valuable because they bring nitrogen, carbon, and oxygen into the air. Clovers are great to plant in the fall; crimson clover is a biennial, so it just grows for a year and it dies out in the spring. If you need them to grow longer you can use red clover or white clover. In the wintertime, we'll grow wheat, rye, and some Austrian winter peas and these cover the ground. You can plant them in September or October and by April they'll be pretty tall. During the first part of May you can plow them in and that adds a lot of organic matter and it's all very helpful.

MW: Have you ever had a plant that surprised you or taught you something about itself that you hadn't known before?

BAREFOOT: Out here, we grow a lot of kale. It over-winters here, and in the spring, it shoots up this flower bud and for years I would think "Well, this plant is flowering; it's becoming bitter and I probably won't eat it." Well, I ate one one day and it was sweet as sugar. I call it "BroKali" now because it's like a little broccoli bud. It is now my favorite vegetable! We've got a whole field of this stuff. Here, let me get you one, they're so good. And to think I went years and didn't even eat them!

(After tasting I can confirm! A delicious crunchy floral kale and broccoli taste).

MW: It tastes like what spring smells like

BAREFOOT: I know! It's better than kale (laughs).

MW: Kale has come under fire lately as an often pesticide-laden product. Where are we headed with this, in terms of the proliferation of chemicals in gardening and farming?

BAREFOOT: First, it would be a good idea to stop using chemicals. The reason to use them in the first place is to concentrate wealth in the hands of the weapons industry. There is no other reason to use them. When you use fertilizer from the chemistry labs, things like ammonium nitrate, super phosphates, potassium chloride, these things disturb the biological activity in natural soil that make those nitrogen, phosphorous, and potassium ions, as they exist naturally, go into the plant. That is done through a symbiotic relationship with fungi and bacteria eating what's coming off of the root; the carbohydrates that stream through the plant are then digested by bacteria and fungi living on the roots of the plant in a healthy, humus-rich soil. Then protozoa eat those and then poop out a readily available amino acid that the plants can then take up that has the minerals that the plant has asked for specifically. There is an interconnection amongst all of the soil microbes. The fungi have hypha that reach out into the soil where there is not even a hard and fast line between where the soil ends and the plant begins; it's all just interconnected activity. Going all the way up, there's things that eat the protozoans, and then there's things that eat those, the earthworms and all the way up to the birds and the mice and the snakes and all of this stuff is moving these nutrients around. Once these things are a biological being, a live being, and that being poops or dies, that's when these nutrients are available for plant growth.

Now when you put chemicals on, then the nitrogen-fixing micro-organisms, who are supposed to be producing this nitrogen for the plant, are essentially living in their own poop, or living in a morgue and they will all die. So there's no potassium-fixing micro-organisms, no phosphorous-mobilizing organisms. The problem becomes: once you start using these chemicals, you have to keep using them. Because if you start using them, six months later your plants are going to start showing chemical deficiency, because you killed the natural processes that were making it all happen. That's why people like Rudolf Steiner said, "Stop using chemicals and go back to farming the way your parents or their parents did for thousands of years."

The soil water becomes full of chemicals, that, while they can make plants grow, the plant doesn't get to choose whether to get those elements naturally or not. It *has* to take it up because it needs water and these chemicals get into the water in the soil. In a natural biological act of the soil, you don't want these elements in the water, you want them to come from natural beings and living things that poop and die. When a plant's leaf wilts, you want it to be able to take up natural water. When a plant is getting nutrients that it hasn't asked for then it grows in an unbalanced way. Nature is really really smart. It has its own ways of noticing whether there is a live, natural humus-rich soil or not. If there is, then nature grows healthy plants, and bugs that you don't want on the plant will fly right by it. I've seen it over and over again; I'll have an acre of potatoes and not have one potato beetle in it. Then I'll look at a potato field down the road and it will be a similar species and it will be full of potato beetles because the soil wasn't good and wasn't being taken care of. It was compacted and hard and not fertilized, like a roadway or something.

What nature does when the soil doesn't have humus, nature says, "Oh my goodness gracious! This soil needs humus! I'll send in my housecleaners!" And the housecleaners are your bugs and diseases. Sometimes you have to be thankful when you lose a crop to bugs because that means nature is taking care of your garden. She's just making more humus for the next crop. We have to let bugs and diseases that naturally befall certain crops be our teachers and help us to understand how these processes work and how we can mimic nature's processes rather than *fight* against it.

MW: Are you optimistic or pessimistic that we might be getting somewhere with all of this, in terms of limiting our dependence on these chemicals and unnatural processes?

BAREFOOT: I'm optimistic because even psychologically, it makes for a better life. It makes more sense to look at the bigger picture and that things are happening for a reason that we don't always understand. The logical thinking would say that chemicals cause cancer and we shouldn't use chemicals. We'll be healthier without them. The idea that we can't grow plants without chemicals is pretty ridiculous because we wouldn't have made it this far if that were true. We have this situation now where in one square foot of ground there is 1,400 pounds of nitrogen in the atmosphere above that. In an acre, there is 70 million pounds of nitrogen above it. For thousands of years, all the nitrogen that was needed for your garden or your farm came from biological processes. To get farmers to start buying nitrogen was a really hard sell. It didn't happen until 30 years after World War II ended that a generation of people had gone through the school systems that had shifted the way they taught agriculture 180 degrees. I have a collection of old farming books from 1914 that clearly explain that you have to make compost, you have to have animals and rotate your pastures and rotate your crops and grow cover crops, put your minerals on the soil, and all these kinds of things that any farmer did. After World War I, the agricultural textbooks started saying, don't have animals and crops on the same farm, because if you do, you're not going to have to buy our fertilizers.

So you had this total shift. Then after the land got depleted of enough of biological activity, they had to supplement the fertilizers with pesticides and things like that because Mother Nature was sending in bugs to make the soil better.

One thing that makes me optimistic is people like you are here, and you're younger and you're asking these questions and you have a garden and you probably won't use chemicals. There's a young man back there who's working and he's asking questions and talking to people and figuring it out. There's certainly a movement going on that's much bigger than when I was young and starting out. But I remember thinking by 1974, every farm would be organic, and we'd be all living off of solar energy. It made logical sense to me. It takes a while to learn that the military-agricultural-industrial complex has a stranglehold on the economy and on education. I'm not saying that we can just fight it and fight it; we just have to work around it, but one of the most revolutionary acts you can do is to grow your own food and eat it.

MW: On a lighter note, you've grown some hops out here on your farm. Has that been a fun project and what advice can you give to the home-hop grower?

BAREFOOT: It started as a project with Yazoo Brewery, one of the first craft breweries in Nashville. I have an English friend who was growing what she called a "hops house" where she

In the "Drink Your Vegetables" chapter (page 150), I talk about the challenges and joys of growing your own celery. The variety we discuss, Tall Utah Celery, was introduced to me by the Barefoot Farmer, who helped us plant some in the garden at Husk. We would only get to experience the joys of Barefoot's celery twice a year, and when we did, there were two drinks that I would focus on:

the Celery Ramos Gin Fizz and a blanco tequila cocktail using the celery tops both for garnish and to make a cordial that would help bring out the bright vegetal notes of the tequila.

CELERY RAMOS GIN FIZZ

3 small celery stalks with leaves, divided
(one top and stem set aside for garnish)

1 dash celery bitters

½ ounce celery cordial
(2 cups chopped celery stems and tops, steeped for
24 hours in a quart of a cold batch of rich simple syrup)

2 ounces Old Tom Gin

⅜ ounce fresh-squeezed lime juice

⅜ ounce fresh-squeezed lemon juice

1 egg white

1 ounce cream

2 drops rosewater (for garnish)

soda water

Add the 2 celery stalks with leaves to your shaking tin, and add the bitters and celery cordial. Muddle to release the aromatics and flavor of the celery. Add the gin, citrus juices, egg white, and cream and dry shake for 30 seconds, without ice, to incorporate the egg white. Add a few large cubes of ice and shake vigorously for a few minutes, if possible (if your arm doesn't fall off first). Double strain into a Collins glass without ice and top with soda water. Garnish by dropping a few drops of rosewater on top and inserting the celery stalk.

THE BAREFOOT GYPSY

6 small celery stalks with leaves,
divided (three set aside for garnish,
to look like a "celery forest")

Tiny pinch (5 to 6 granules) Maldon sea salt

¼ ounce Grenadine
(equal parts pomegranate juice and sugar,
heated and stirred to combine)

¼ ounce orange blossom honey syrup
(2 parts honey to 1 part water,
stirred to combine)

2 ounces Blanco Tequila

¾ ounce fresh-squeezed lime juice

½ ounce Cynar

Muddle 3 of the celery stalks with leaves, along
with the salt, grenadine and orange blossom honey
at the bottom of a shaker tin. Add the remaining
ingredients, (reserving 3 celery stalks and tops
for garnish) and shake vigorously with ice. Double
strain into a Collins glass or Mason jar filled halfway with ice. Garnish with the 3 celery stalks.

was growing hops over a lattice structure. I got some root cuttings from her and started growing them, and eventually, I had grown a truckload of hops. So Linus, the brewmaster from Yazoo Brewery, came out and filled up the back of his truck and took them back to his brewery. He was able to use them in some of his different beers, and next thing you know, he's got beer with local hops. Now, I never really got paid for that, but if I go into Yazoo Brewery when I'm in Nashville, they usually give me a beer (laughs). I'd love to be able to supply him completely with a bunch of hops but the best hops grow in Washington and the Northwest. Just like really good grapes grow in California and so on. I don't think California and Washington can grow as good of a sweet potato that we can grow in Tennessee and that's just how it goes. Different areas have different things that they're known for. I don't know the exact reason, it's just a matter of environment and climate, but this isn't really the best area for hops. They are easy to grow though. And what's amazing about these kinds of things is it may take a long time for us to stumble on a different variety or something mutates, and we realize you can actually grow really good hops in Tennessee. We're always learning, and it never really stops. Hops are a great example of that. To start though, getting a handle on what *does* grow well in your area can give you an idea of what you want to start with. I do in-season, easy-to-grow vegetables.

CHAPTER

4

RHUBARB, REDBUD, & THE SPRING BLING

The grass outside is still cold, an earthy yellow with little flecks of green, like a punk rocker's hairdo. Looking closer, heart-shaped green leaves abound throughout the yard and garden, soon to give way to bursts of purple, as violets bloom and lend the air a perfume-like sweet fragrance that smells faintly of birthday cake. Dandelions roar open and stretch their blossoms like hundreds of little suns growing taller by the day until they're teed up like golf balls, to be smacked by the wind, blowing seeds back into the earth to start the whole dance back up again. Field garlic "chives" dart up through the grass, growing twice as fast, until that first mow when the whole yard smells like garlic pesto. Redbud trees show off their pink and red blossoms, so harmonious they appear purple if you drive by fast enough, signaling that this spring thing is really *on*, as the neighborhood turns from stark and tangled to vibrant and inspired. Forsythia's overflowing branches light up the block like a golden Christmas tree—you know, the one that's still sitting in your backyard from a few months ago, shrinking into an old brown stogie just begging for an early spring bonfire.

In the garden, signs of life are sprouting up everywhere, from the lemon balm you cut back in November, to the mint that is plotting its own renovations, poised to come back stronger and take up twice as much space as last year. Maybe that's all right. But maybe, you'll have to start planning on how to keep that mint from taking over your entire herb garden (more on this later). If you're lucky enough to have a rhubarb plant or two, spring is rhubarb's time to shine, and seeing a small planet of rhubarb beginning to unfurl from the soil is one of the ultimate joys of gardening. It's often the first thing you'll notice in your spring garden carrying over from last year, even before any buds appear on the trees. It's a beautiful, welcome sight. And before the heat sets in, those tart, juicy stalks make for great syrups and tonics, shrubs, and Rhubarb Crisp desserts, and can be peeled for elegant cocktail garnishes. Before we get to sipping a Spring Collins out on the porch on that

first 65-degree day, we'll make some rhubarb elixirs perfect for all kinds of cocktails and nonalcoholic beverages. First, let's discuss some basic parameters for growing rhubarb—and if you're renting, you may want to renew your lease first.

RHUBARB: THE ETERNAL TONIC

Rhubarb has long been one of those vegetables that is fun and engaging for first-time gardeners, though it does require a little patience. The best way to get started is to purchase one-year crowns from your favorite garden store or nursery, and pick out a spot in your garden that has a little afternoon shade. Rhubarb prefers mostly full sun, but doesn't enjoy extreme heat, so it's best to find some balance between full sun and part shade. It can be planted in the earliest days of spring, or late in the fall, after dormancy has set in. You'll be surprised how big rhubarb plants can grow, so take care to space them out by 3 to 4 feet, depending on the varietal you're growing. For those beautiful, streaking red stalks, I recommend a red variety like Tilden, Crimson, or Valentine. Red varieties are often more tender than their green counterparts as well, so they will yield more of that round, robust flavor when used in infusions. Rhubarb is a hungry plant, so be sure to mix in a lot of organic matter and compost to give your plant a good foundation to thrive. Mulch regularly with organic materials such as dried grass clippings (be certain they haven't been sprayed with herbicide), chopped leaves, newspaper, compost, and rotted hay. This will help retain moisture for the thirsty rhubarb plants and help keep weeds away. Rhubarb needs some time to establish its strong stalks, so harvesting during the first season isn't recommended, though to be honest, I haven't been able to resist when I've started rhubarb plants. Some other don'ts regarding rhubarb: *don't* use the leaves or flowers. The leaves contain high concentrations of oxalic acid, which can be toxic if ingested. The flowers are also toxic and don't contain any magical rhubarb flavor with which to garnish your perfect late-spring Strawberry Daiquiri. We're only after those juicy stalks, which can be lightly twisted and pulled away from the base of the plant when the stalk is one to two feet long. To keep the individual plants healthy, the *Farmer's Almanac* recommends leaving at least two healthy stalks on each plant at all times. As fall and winter settle in, the stalks will begin to die, but fear not: Simply cut them back, cover with mulch, and wait for those burgeoning buds to come back to life in early spring. That's another reason why picking out a good location for rhubarb in your garden is so important. With a little care (it needs to be divided every 5 to 8 years), it will come back every year and fill you with so much joy when it announces, "Springtime is coming!" And since the crown comes back stronger every year and produces more stalks, you're going to have to get creative to use up all that rhubarb.

Rhubarb is native to Siberia and has been used medicinally throughout Asia for thousands of years. The purgative power of these early rhubarb varieties was so revered in Chinese medicine and throughout Asia, Europe, and Russia that the plant was used as a diplomatic tool amid disputes between bickering kingdoms. In 1759, the Quianlong emperor of the Qing dynasty forbid the export of tea and rhubarb to Russia after a border conflict in Northern China. Italians began planting rhubarb and using it for culinary purposes throughout the eighteenth century, and "Chinese rhubarb," a way of saying "the good medicinal stuff," was used in many early vermouth and chinato recipes and is still used today. If you inspect the beautifully unique packaging for Cocchi Barolo Chinato, a triangular box with depictions of key ingredients on one side, you'll notice "Chinese rhubarb" as one of the ingredients. By the nineteenth century, the Chinese government, keenly aware of how popular it was throughout Britain, threatened to withhold all exports of rhubarb if British merchants did not stop trading in opium. Some historians suggest the Opium War—let's face it, an intriguing name for a war if there ever was one—should actually have been called the Rhubarb War.

SPRING TONIC

4 quarts water

1 cup dried sarsaparilla or sassafras root
(sassafras will give you more of a cinnamon flavor)

2 cups dandelion flowers, pinched from their stems

2 cups chopped rhubarb stalks
(chopped into 2-inch pieces)

2 cups honey

In a pot, bring the water to a boil, then lower the heat a little to a hard simmer, add the sarsaparilla or sassafras, and cook, covered, for 10 minutes. Next, add the dandelion and rhubarb and lower the heat to a low simmer. Let the ingredients simmer together for 30 to 45 minutes, covered. Add the honey to your tonic and stir to incorporate. Strain, cool, and enjoy hot or over ice. This mixture will keep in the fridge, covered, for a week.

In the United States, if you happen to be lucky enough to live in a mountainous area, such as the Rocky Mountains, where rhubarb begins to shoot up at the tail end of a short spring season, you may be able to find it in abundance all around you. Many of the largest rhubarb plants in the world reside in Alaska, where descendants of the plants grown in the early 1900s by gardener Henry Clark, known as the Rhubarb King, still grow to this day. One thing is for sure: rhubarb will outlive us all.

Settlers and natives of the Americas did not, as it turned out, share very well, but one tradition they both engaged in, as if compelled by the stifling colder months, was that of spring tonics. Believed to spur circulation and prepare the body for the coming work of spring, these tonics can still have a place in our drinking routine today. Many early tonic recipes involved gathering whatever wild herbs and greens would first pop up at the beginning of spring, boiling them in water, and drinking the resulting liquid, known as "potlikker." Dandelion was a popular ingredient for many of these spring tonics, and we use its floral, honeyed, bittersweet magic alongside rhubarb in our Spring Tonic.

For centuries, rhubarb has been known as the "pie plant," and it is a phenomenal dessert ingredient for one reason: it's begging for sugar, at least to our raised-on-Coca-Cola palates. Rhubarb contains oxalic acid, which gives the stalks that tart, sour pop that squeezes your cheeks like Aunt Millie. As mentioned previously, the leaves contain so much oxalic acid that they can be poisonous, and are therefore never to be used. These tart and acidic sensibilities also make rhubarb a perfect ingredient for syrups and cordials. But there's another ingredient, in addition to sugar, that we'll want to have on hand when using rhubarb: angelica. Whether in fresh or dried form, this often hard-to-find herb with a very subtle fennel/licorice flavor shares many of the beautifully complex flavors of rhubarb and helps to integrate the flavor of rhubarb into cocktails.

RHUBARB-ANGELICA
CORDIAL

8 cups water

8 cups sugar

4 cups chopped rhubarb stalks
(chopped into 1-inch segments)

½ cup dried angelica

1 cinnamon stick, crushed

1 teaspoon whole cloves

Zest of 2 lemons

1 cup fresh angelica leaves and stalks
(if available; stalks peeled)

Combine the water and sugar in a pot and bring to a near-boil, stirring to incorporate the sugar. When the mixture comes to a hard simmer, turn down the heat to a medium simmer, add the rhubarb, dried angelica, cinnamon, and cloves, and stir to incorporate. Simmer the mixture for 20 minutes, then add the lemon zest and remove from the heat to cool. Once the syrup has completely cooled, add the fresh angelica, if you have some available. If you're not able to procure some, don't let it keep you from making this delicious elixir, but adding the fresh leaves and stalks from the angelica will introduce a vibrant herbaceous quality to the syrup that will help it stand out in cocktails and nonalcoholic drinks. Transfer the syrup to the refrigerator and let the ingredients infuse for 2 to 3 days, tasting the syrup each day to see how strong it is. When it tastes strong and dynamically flavored with rhubarb and angelica, strain the mixture through a tea strainer or chinois, bottle it, and keep it in the refrigerator. If using fresh angelica, save the strained stalks to make Candied Angelica (page 90). In the refrigerator, the syrup will keep for a few months.

So many of the exotic liqueurs of the world with closely held secret recipes are said to contain angelica, including Chartreuse, Fernet, Benedictine, and many classic amaros; it's a wonder the ingredient isn't used behind the bar more often. It also shares an affinity with juniper and is used as a key element in many gins around the world, specifically London dry gins and Old Tom styles, making it a perfect ingredient for gin cocktails (see chapter 5, "Gin for the Win") Angelica has been held in such high esteem throughout history that it is also known as the "Root of the Holy Spirit." Legend has it the herb received its name because it was brought to a monk in a dream by an angel, who told him it would cure the plague. Another monk would later say, and I'm paraphrasing, "That sounds great, but I think I'll just make some Chartreuse with it." The Iroquois Indians used it as ceremonial medicine, and it has long been used by many cultures to ward off evil spirits. Since many garden stores and nurseries don't sell angelica plants (bless them if they do!) you can find seeds online and begin to grow them from seed. You'll need to give angelica plenty of space, since the plants can grow up to six feet tall, and it will provide some possibly unwanted shade to plants that grow around it. Be very careful if you plan on looking for angelica in the wild. It shares some characteristics with poison hemlock and can, to the untrained eye, be mistaken for hemlock for a few reasons: both share a hairless, purple stem (though hemlock's is spotted purple) and both have Queen Anne's lace–like umbels of flowers, though angelica's flowers are an earthy yellow-green. If growing angelica is going to take up too much space in your garden, you can purchase the dried stem and root at some home brew stores and online to pair with rhubarb in a spring cordial.

Since angelica remains such a key ingredient in so many gins, we're going to put the Rhubarb-Angelica Cordial to use in a classic gin cocktail "template," using a gin known to contain and showcase the wonders of angelica. Plymouth Navy Strength Gin is the answer to your prayer, "Plymouth Gin is so amazing, I just wish

SPRING RHUBARB COLLINS

I large rhubarb stalk, divided

Juice from I lemon (¾ to I ounce)

¾ ounce Rhubarb-Angelica Cordial (page 86)

5 fresh angelica leaves
(optional), plus more for garnish

1½ ounces Plymouth Navy Strength Gin

I ounce Spring Tonic (page 84)

Soda water
(preferably Mountain Valley
Sparkling Mineral Water or Topo Chico)

Candied Angelica
(optional, recipe follows), for garnish

Cut two 2-inch pieces of rhubarb, and set the rest of the stalk aside for garnish. Place the rhubarb pieces in a large glass (how large depends on how long you want to sit on your porch without getting up to make another—if your glass is Big Gulp-worthy, go ahead and double the recipe). Add the lemon juice, cordial, and, if available, the angelica. Muddle this mixture, taking care not to smash the herbs to smithereens. Add the gin and the spring tonic and fill the glass half-full with ice. Stir everything together to incorporate, top with a little more ice, then add your soda water to fill the glass. That wasn't so hard, was it? Add your large stalk of rhubarb to swizzle away the rest of your afternoon, and garnish with some angelica, using either a few fresh leaves, the flowers, or some candied angelica, which can be used as a straw.

it weren't so subtle, pretty, and light! Is there anything this tasty that is so strong, I can make a supersize Tom Collins, and not have to get my ass off of this porch swing for at least an hour or two?"

"Let there be Plymouth Navy Strength!" the gods declared with the fervor of sailors. "But don't say I didn't warn thee! It can smacketh thine own face with its power!"

The Tom Collins is just the template we're looking for to showcase both our rhubarb cordial and the rhubarb and angelica we've got on hand for garnish. Simply put, the Tom Collins is gin, the juice of one lemon, a few spoonfuls of sugar, and a good topping of soda water, served in a tall glass with a straw. It's a simple, refreshing cocktail that, in the hot months of summer, can go down all too fast. It's an incredibly easy template to use to mix and match different flavors, spirits, and ingredients; one could go an entire summer making nothing but Collins variations (tequila-lime-pineapple soda Collins, anyone?) and drink very well. It's also a drink that doesn't require bar tools. It can be nice to shake up that mixture of gin, lemon, and sugar, carefully straining it into a glass and topping it with artisanal soda, but with this cocktail and its devil-may-care attitude, it is definitely not necessary. Sometimes the toughest decision with a Collins variation is deciding which soda to use. Generally, you're either getting your dynamic flavors from the spirit-syrup combo or from a potent mixture of spirit and a good soda, which can more than make up for the sugar. So if you're using a flavor bomb soda like Jarritos grapefruit soda, you won't need any other sugar for the drink itself.

This rhubarb-angelica variation is the drink you think about all day while you're busy getting the garden ready for summer. This drink is your reward: mix one up and go wind down the evening, listening for the first crickets and searching for that annual spark of light from the first firefly.

CANDIED ANGELICA

If you were able to use fresh angelica for the Rhubarb-Angelica Cordial, then you've got a major head start on making Candied Angelica, which makes for a great cocktail garnish, a whimsical drinking straw, and an even more palatable way to get the health benefits of angelica. The reason we peeled the angelica before making the cordial (page 86) is to maintain as much of the vibrant fresh angelica flavor as possible. For this recipe, we'll peel after blanching to make the process a little easier.

I quart angelica stems and stalks

2 cups water

2 cups sugar

Superfine sugar, for coating

salt

water

I Tablespoon of salt and 4 quarts of water
(for blanching the angelica)

Cut the angelica into pieces the size of drinking straws. Prepare an ice bath and set aside. Bring a pot of salted water to a hard simmer, add the angelica, and blanch for 3 to 4 minutes, then dunk the angelica into the ice bath to cool. Meanwhile, combine the water and sugar in a pot and cook, stirring until the sugar has dissolved. As your syrup heats up, take the stems and stalks out of the ice bath, peel the very outer layer of each one, and toss them in the syrup. Let the syrup come to a boil, then lower the heat to a medium simmer, cooking the stems for 20 minutes. Remove the pot from the heat, cover, and let the angelica stems infuse into the syrup overnight, at room temp. After 24 hours or so of infusion time, remove the stems, roll them in superfine sugar, and let them dry on a cooling rack for a few days, at room temp. Store the candied angelica in an airtight container in the fridge, or away from sunlight in a cupboard, labeled and dated. They will keep for a month.

THE ALPINE DIGESTIF

If you prefer to drink your dessert, or have eaten such a large meal that the thought of forcing down a big piece of cheesecake sounds like work, try this cooling, herbaceous delight using your new, crystalline candied angelica: A few hours ahead of time, place a bottle of génépy, the French Alpine liqueur that tastes of Chartreuse on Christmas morning, into the freezer (that's where it should be anyway) to chill thoroughly. Now, pour a shot of frozen génépy into a small glass and garnish with a stick of candied angelica. Sip the génépy through the candied angelica "straw," taking little bites out of your straw to blend the flavors of the angelica and the génépy. This makes for a very satisfying end to a meal, and will aid in digestion.

IN PRAISE OF THE PROLIFERATE POLLINATORS

Though we've covered the mighty dandelion (page 38), a plant so smart it only requires a little wind to spread its seed near and far (though it *could* use a marketing director), there are many other flowers that are equally delicious when made into cordials and liqueurs once spring has initially sprung. And like our friend the dandelion, many of these plants are not only useful for culinary and medicinal purposes, but also are one of the earliest sources of spring nectar for bees and butterflies. The easiest way to help these spring pollinators is by putting the pesticides away and letting nature take its course. If you want to take it a step further, and to make you feel better for using some of those dandelions in our Dandelion Cordial (page 44), here are five other plants to assist pollinators, which also happen to be beneficial for your garden as a whole:

* Borage

* Bee Balm

* Chives

* African Blue Basil

* Calendula

These multi-faceted, majestic plants have a lot to offer in a culinary sense as well. You can make cordials and show-stopping garnishes out of these herbs (chives work well in Bloody Marys, for example, and are essential for the home cook), and all are very easy to grow.

Violet and forsythia are two spring pollinator-friendly plants that grow in abundance in zones 3 through 9, and offer the professional bartender or the home enthusiast elegant flavors to work with. Adding a "floral" note to a cocktail can be a challenging task without overpowering the drink: Orange blossom water is a great tool for drinks and cordials, but it can overwhelm when added to just one drink, and rosewater, which I love, can also quickly make a badass drink suddenly seem like tea in grandma's living room. Violet and forsythia are much subtler and more readily available options for adding a delicate floral note. Both plants arrive on the scene around the same time of the year, though forsythia is usually early to the party. Another springtime fixture native to China, forsythia is quite easy to identify in early spring. Look for the flashes of light yellow, turning gold in the early sunset, which emanate from leafless branches. The leaves come later and are generally not eaten unless very young. The flowers have a pleasant bitterness, similar to but much lighter than dandelion greens, providing an interesting contrast with the floral character they give to a cordial. While there are numerous ways to add the all-important "bitterness" to bitters, including dried gentian root, dried wormwood, and other packaged bittering agents, forsythia provides a uniquely

SPRING FLOWERS BITTERS

1 dandelion root

2 handfuls of fresh forsythia blossoms

1 handful of fresh violet blossoms

5 fresh dandelion flowers

5 honeysuckle blossoms

2 Queen Anne's Lace flower heads
(be sure you can identify;
look for a hairy stem and a carrot-like aroma)

2 sprigs of thyme

1 sprig of rosemary

1 tablespoon dried iris root
(orris root)

Zest of 1 lemon

Zest of 1 orange

100 proof vodka,
a little less than 32 ounces
so as not to crowd the Mason jar
you're infusing into

2 tablespoons orange blossom honey

Preheat the oven to 200°F. Wash the dandelion root and roast it for 40 minutes, then cool to room temperature. Place the root in a 32-ounce Mason jar and add the rest of the flowers, herbs, roots, and zests. Fill the jar with vodka, leaving an inch of space at the top. Put the cap on and store the jar in a cool, dark place away from sunlight for 1 week, shaking it a few times a day. After a week, add the honey, shake to incorporate, and leave it for another week, shaking periodically. After 2 weeks, strain and bottle. The bitters will keep for months, in a shady spot in the kitchen away from sunlight.

VIOLET CORDIAL

1 quart organic sugar

1 pint water

1 teaspoon citric acid

1 quart lightly packed purple violets,
picked in mid-morning and lightly washed

1 teaspoon dried iris root (orris root)

Zest of 1 lemon

1 sprig of lavender (optional)

Combine the sugar, water, and citric acid in a pot
and cook at a low simmer, stirring to incorporate
and dissolve the sugar. Remove from the heat and
let cool to nearly room temperature. Once the syrup
has cooled, add the violets, iris root, lemon zest,
and lavender, and refrigerate. Let the cordial infuse
in the refrigerator for a few days, ideally adding
more violets picked in mid-morning during that
time. (To allow the violet flavor to come through in
cocktails, you're going to need a lot of blossoms.)
When you're happy with the flavor, strain out the
solids, being careful not to agitate the ingredients
to avoid clouding the cordial. Stored in the refrigerator, it will keep for around a month.

fresh floral snap to bitters recipes. Spring is an ideal time to make bitters, because there are so many fresh bittering options available.

We'll use these incomparable bitters in a spring pisco (Peruvian brandy) drink, but first we'll gather more violets and make a home-made batch of crème de violette, famous for its inclusion in the classic cocktail, the Aviation. Just as St. Germain doesn't *completely* capture the flavor of elderflower, most commercial crème de violettes don't taste much like pure violet. But there's a good reason for that. The flavor is so fleeting it must be captured immediately in mid-morning, after the blossoms have opened and before the afternoon sun and wind have partially dried the aroma. The goal is to pick as many as you can, wash them lightly in cold water, and immediately plunge them into a warm-to-room-temperature rich simple syrup. Boiling the flowers will dull the flavor and muddy the color. One of the tricks to working with violets is to also use dried iris root, or orris root (made from *Iris Germanica* and *Iris Pallida*), which has a fresh, violet-like aroma, along with some bitterness, and is used in many gin and vermouth recipes.

While Aviations—gin, lemon, crème de violette, and maraschino liqueur—are the time-honored classic cocktail of choice for violets, I enjoy pairing pisco, a grape brandy with an unmistakable floral note, with all manner of spring ingredients. Pisco has more character, flavor, and viscosity than vodka, and it won't overwhelm delicate botanicals like violet and forsythia.

As in nature, after the flower comes the berry, so next we'll look at the coming summer fruits, particularly berries, as well as the rush of herbs and, eventually, vegetables, which all offer their own ways to enrich the drinking experience for the gardener, the guest, and the home bartender.

JET TO MACCHU PICCHU

(THE PISCO AVIATION)

2 ounces Peruvian pisco,
such as Pisco 100

½ ounce lemon juice

¾ ounce Violet Cordial (page 94)

1 bar spoon (⅛ ounce) lime juice

2 dashes Spring Flowers Bitters (page 93)

3 to 4 small needles of lavender

Edible spring flowers, for garnish

Combine pisco, citrus juices, cordial, bitters, and lavender in a shaker tin with ice. Shake until well chilled and strain into a coupe glass. Garnish with violets, forsythia, or any other edible vibrant spring flower, as long as you are able to identify it.

CHAPTER

5

A BOUNTY OF BERRIES

& Gin for the Win

I n spring, before the beloved blackberry and blueberry bounty make their way to the market, another berry is out there, often unnoticed yet so crucial to the world of cocktails: the juniper berry. While fall is the ideal time to forage for wild juniper berries, making sure that you harvest the most widely available juniper variety, the aptly named Common Juniper, spring and summer offer so many ingredients to choose from and they all seem to go well with gin. You can even make your own gin, using dried juniper berries, some spices from the pantry that you totally forgot about, like that dried orris root some crazy bartender told you to buy (page 95) and in-season botanicals like the first burst of lemon balm in your garden. I've taught training classes for bartenders and servers who are interested in gin and the last thing we do, to better visualize that gin is basically one big infusion of fresh and dried ingredients, is to make a big batch of homemade gin.

CONSIDER THE MARTINI

Since we're talking about gin, the spirit that can smack your palate awake, and tickle the senses with its aromatic witchcraft, suitable for classics and modern updates alike, I feel like we must discuss the simple pleasures of the martini. My wife, Kate, bless her E.R.-nurse-lifesaving heart, never knew how much she loved dry martinis until she actually had a proper one. And for the purposes of this book, and life in general, dry martini means *gin* martini, cold as Chicago in January martini, herbaceous and vivacious martini, good for any season or reason martini. Before we dive into the late spring into summer headrush of beautiful berries and plentiful herbs growing in the garden, practically all of which pair well with gin, let's get the simple joys of the martini out into the open. The difference between a good martini and a transcendent one is often a matter of how all the tiny details come together before the drink is poured into the glass. Sure, the actual recipe and ratios matter, but this drink is a perfect example of how process and method can

GARDEN GIN

2 (750 ml) bottles of vodka

1 cup dried juniper berries
(or a little less if you're one of those
"I drink gin but don't like juniper as much,"
weirdos)

1 tablespoon dried orris (iris) root

1 handful of fresh violet flowers

5 fresh dandelion flowers

Zest from 1 lime

Zest from 1 lemon

1 tablespoon pink peppercorns

10 lemon balm leaves

1 sprig of mint

1 sprig of rosemary

1 sprig of lavender

Add all ingredients to a large sealable container and stir to incorporate. Seal and let it sit for a week at room temperature, shaking or agitating the mixture daily. After a week, taste the batch and see if it can benefit from any other ingredients you may have at your disposal, like honeysuckle or wisteria flowers. If you'd like a stronger, more juniper-forward gin, simply add more juniper (¼ cup to ½ cup), stir to incorporate, and allow the batch to sit for one more week. After 2 weeks, strain the gin through a fine mesh strainer and bottle. Kept in a shady spot at room temperature, the gin will keep for 3 to 6 months.

be even more important than ratios, which can often be subjective. If you can make a proper martini, you can take that knowledge and put it to use in so many other drinks, as it forces you to think about the little things that make an excellent drink. In the case of the martini, those little things include a properly chilled glass, avoiding the temptation to over-stir, and garnishing wisely. A lemon twist-olive combo is classic, but you can also take the opportunity to use a small piece of herbal decoration from the garden. A small sprig of rosemary, lavender, thyme, or sage can provide that extra aromatic "pop" that makes a martini memorable. So if you've got some fragrant powerhouses beginning to spread in the garden, possibly some lemon balm or lemon verbena, this is a great drink to add a little herbaceous accent at the finish. Lastly, adjust your recipe as needed to account for the amount of juniper in the gin. For a bold gin like beefeater, try 2 to 2¼ ounces of gin per serving; for a lighter gin like Plymouth (one of my personal faves), you may want to use more so it won't get overpowered by the vermouth. Oh, and go ahead and use that new Garden Gin too!

Without further ado...

THE GARDEN TO GLASS MARTINI

2 to 3 ounces gin, to taste

½ ounce to 1 ounce of French dry vermouth
(like Dolin or La Quintinye Royal, which is exquisite)

1 dash orange, lemon,
or Spring Flower Bitters (page 93)

Garden herbs, such as lemon balm,
lemon verbena, or rosemary

Good olives, for garnish

Lemon twist, for garnish

soda water

Fill a mixing glass or pint glass with very cold water to chill it, or put it in the refrigerator or freezer while you prepare the other ingredients. While the mixing glass gets cold, prepare the martini glass by filling it with ice and soda water or by placing it in the freezer to thoroughly chill. When the outside of the mixing glass is cold, dump out the water and fill the mixing glass three-quarters full of ice. Add the gin, vermouth, and bitters and stir briskly for 15 seconds. Add a few herbs, reserving some for garnish, and stir a few more revolutions to incorporate them. Add a few more ice cubes on top and let the drink sit, allowing the herbs to infuse for 5 minutes. Walk away from it and prepare your garnish by cutting a piece of fresh herb, putting a few olives on a pick, and finding your channel knife for the all-important lemon twist. After 5 minutes, taste the martini to be sure it's as cold as possible. Wait a few more minutes if it's not. Don't stir it.

Retrieve the prepared martini glass from the freezer or dump out the soda and ice. Add the olives to the empty chilled glass and strain the martini into the glass. Twist a lemon over the top, then perch the twist on the side of the glass. Add a sprig of herb from the garden for aromatic punch. Consider the mysteries of life, and drink to them! Cheers!

BRAMBLES AND BERRIES & BOOZE

Like the martini, the bramble, made with gin, blackberry, and lemon, is one of those classic gin drinks that has stood the test of time. However, when fresh local berries begin to hit the market in my home of Middle Tennessee, the bramble cocktail begs to be expanded on. No cocktail is better-suited for summer bounty than the bramble, but I look at those three powerhouse ingredients and realize there's one thing missing: herbs. Especially the potent, lemon-flavored herbs like lemon balm and lemon verbena. These herbs, with their citrusy aroma and flavor, go well with almost any style of gin; in fact, they are even used in the recipes for some gins, like Colorado's Dry Town Gin and Monkey 47.

Lemon balm and lemon verbena are easy to grow, and can be harvested frequently to encourage more vigorous growth. Lemon balm can be especially robust and should be given plenty of space when planted. The fragrant leaves and pretty white flowers are great for making tea, cordials, and garnishes, and for use in lemonade and iced tea recipes (page 137). Lemon verbena, one of my all-time favorite herbs, can be a little more challenging to grow, but its unique flavor—like pink peppercorns and thyme mixed with the skin of a green pepper—and its strong lemon peel aroma make it indispensable in the garden. It's a flavor that just can't be replicated. And there's a good reason to grow your own lemon verbena: it's quite hard to find fresh at markets, and the starter plants are usually snatched up fast at nurseries in the spring. It is native to South America and enjoys a more equatorial climate, so plant it in a sunny spot in your garden in soil with good drainage. The roots need plenty of space and do not tolerate being waterlogged, especially in early spring and late fall when the temperature drops. Lemon verbena can be pruned confidently in late spring and early summer, which increases production and gives you plenty of delicious leaves later in the summer and into fall.

LEMON HERB BRAMBLE NO. 1

½ lemon, ends removed, quartered

5 leaves lemon balm, divided

4 leaves lemon verbena, divided

4 fresh, ripe blackberries, divided

½ ounce simple syrup
(made with organic sugar)

Scant pinch of salt

2 ounces citrus-forward gin,
like Malfey's Lemon Gin

Combine the lemon, 3 lemon balm leaves, 3 lemon verbena leaves, 2 blackberries, the simple syrup, and the salt in a shaker tin and muddle together thoroughly, taking care not to brutalize the herbs. Use just enough pressure to release the oils in the citrus and blend them with the oils from the herbs and the fruit from the blackberries. The syrup will help mix the ingredients together. Pouring the gin over the muddler and into the tin, thus washing off any ingredients stuck to the muddler. Add ice and shake until well chilled and frosty cold. Double strain the drink into a rocks glass or tumbler over ice, and reinforce the herbal flavor by garnishing with the remaining lemon balm, lemon verbena, and fresh blackberries. Summer in a glass!

A perfect herb for liquid application, lemon verbena is relatively toothsome and works best as the star of an infusion or as the aromatic citrus-pop garnish in a gin and tonic, gimlet, gin sour—or, of course, a bramble. The verbena's hint of spice, almost anise-like, complements blackberries so well, you'll want to use it in blackberry cobbler and other desserts as well as in this blackberry-based cocktail. A traditional bramble uses Crème de Mure, a French blackberry liqueur. But since blackberries are plentiful in summertime, it's only natural to use fresh blackberries, both to muddle in the drink and for garnish. We'll look at two ways to make this ideal summer cocktail, using fresh ingredients and a smash method for one application, and making your own Blackberry-Herb Liqueur for the other, which allows you to stretch the blackberry season a little longer. Any citrus-forward gin, like Malfey's Gin from Italy (try their Lemon Gin for a lemon bomb!), would be a great choice for this drink.

If blackberry season is more fleeting in your area, or if you'd like to pick your own blackberries in the wild and stretch them out, you can preserve their flavor by making a blackberry liqueur. Picking blackberries can be a thorny endeavor, though a safe one as there aren't any poisonous look-alikes. As with all foraging you just want to be sure no pesticides have been sprayed in the area. Also check for orange and brown-spotted blackberry leaves, as that can indicate fungal problems in the blackberry patch. Picking blackberries yourself affords you the opportunity to also gather some leaves, which have been used in teas traditionally and are recognized in Germany for health benefits ranging from diarrhea relief to helping with sore throats (always consult with your doctor first). If using the leaves, pick only young leaves and use them either fresh or completely dried. Another benefit of picking your own is that you'll be able to taste the big difference between the plump, sweet ripe berries and the more acidic, vegetal unripened berries, which gives you a different side of the blackberry to explore. Just as unripened

LEMON HERB BLACKBERRY LIQUEUR

1 quart ripened blackberries

1 quart organic sugar

1 pint water

2 cinnamon sticks,
crushed with the back of a skillet

6 cloves

¼ cup fresh young blackberry leaves

Juice and peel of 1 lemon,
with as little pith as possible

1 cup vodka

1 tablespoon green Chartreuse (optional)

1 tablespoon yellow Chartreuse (optional)

½ cup lemon balm leaves

½ cup lemon verbena leaves

Heat a nonreactive pot over low heat; add the blackberries, and lightly muddle them to release some of their juices. Add the sugar, water, crushed cinnamon, cloves, and blackberry leaves and bring to a gentle simmer. Cover and simmer the syrup for 10 minutes, then promptly remove from the heat and let cool. Once the mixture has cooled, add the lemon juice and peels, vodka, and Chartreuse, if using (both the green and yellow Chartreuse are optional, but if you have them available, they complement the herbal kick of the lemon herbs well). Lightly muddle the lemon balm and verbena and add them to the cooled elixir. Allow the ingredients to infuse overnight in the refrigerator. Taste the homemade liqueur the following day and let it steep longer if you'd like a stronger flavor. When the flavor is strong enough, strain out the solids and bottle. With the amount of vodka in this liqueur, it will taste best from the refrigerator, where it can be kept for months.

LEMON HERB BRAMBLE NO. 2

2 ounces citrus-forward gin
(try Tanqueray 10 or Citadelle)

¾ ounce lemon juice

¾ ounce Lemon Herb Blackberry Liqueur

1 dash Angostura bitters

Scant pinch of salt

Lemon balm leaves,
lemon verbena leaves,
and fresh blackberries, for garnish

Combine the gin, lemon juice, liqueur, Angostura bitters, and salt in a shaker tin, add ice, and shake, until well chilled. Roll (pouring everything from the shaker including the ice) into a rocks glass and garnish with the lemon herbs and blackberries. Float a little of your homemade blackberry liqueur on top.

grapes are used to make tart, acidic verjus, you can use unripened blackberries to spur your culinary imagination and provide yourself with a unique tool to add acid to dishes. When fully ripened, blackberries become quite glossy in appearance, turning darker by the day as the fruit inside becomes juicier.

If growing berries is of interest to you and you've got the space, blackberries are the most plentiful option, as one bramble of blackberries can produce up to 20 pounds of fruit. They will grow vigorously and enjoy plenty of space to stretch out and get comfortable. However, if they aren't contained in some way by a border or a hedge, they will grow unwieldy and can take over a space. To decide between thorned or thornless blackberries there are a few things to consider. For starters, how many cuts do you want on your arms, and how much fruit will you be using? If you anticipate wanting to have as many blackberries as possible, thorned varieties produce a lot of fruit (and produce it earlier than thornless varieties), and they can keep producing throughout the summer and fall. Thornless berries are a little more easygoing and are obviously easier to maintain, though they usually require trellising, whereas thorned varieties don't. There are different varieties of brambles that work well in different growing zones, so it's best to research or ask your local nursery which varieties they've had success with.

Strawberries are also relatively easy to grow and do quite well in large pots, whiskey barrel planters, or, if space is an issue, even in smaller pots sitting on a sunny porch or balcony. Strawberries have a smaller root system than other berries and can therefore thrive in less space. Keep in mind, the deeper the pot you use to grow your strawberries, the less water they'll need. Using a smaller container means you'll have to keep a closer watch on them to keep them hydrated. Allow strawberries to go dormant in the winter, watering only occasionally when the soil is very dry, and keep in mind that you'll probably need to replace strawberry plants every three years or so. If you live in an area with very cold winters, dormant strawberry pots can be brought into a shed or a garage for dormancy or brought indoors if space permits.

There are many ways to approach using strawberries in cocktails, whether by muddling them, using them for garnish as in a traditional Sherry Cobbler (page 55), or making shrubs, cordials, and teas with the fruit, leaves, and strawberry tops. One thing is certain: you definitely want to use those tops and stems, don't simply cut them off and discard them. They have medicinal value in their own right, with vitamins and nutrients all their own, and the tannins in the tops and leaves can help aid with digestion. They also taste mildly of parsley, something you can bolster by adding a few leaves of parsley to your strawberry concoctions. And if you know you'll be using a strawberry cordial with lime juice in a cocktail or nonalcoholic drink, adding lime juice and zest to the cordial recipe can be an effective way to build big flavors in your drinks.

STRAWBERRY CORDIAL

2 quarts strawberries with tops,
quartered

2 quarts sugar

2 quarts water

Zest of 1 orange

Zest of 1 lemon

1 ounce lemon juice

1 pinch of salt
(optional, to tame the sweetness
of overripe strawberries)

Combine all the ingredients in a pot and bring to a simmer. Let simmer for about 30 minutes, then remove from the heat and let sit to infuse for a few days in the refrigerator. Strain out the solids after 2 to 3 days and bottle the cordial.

Strawberries also go very well with the aforementioned aperitivos of Italy, like Aperol and Campari, and they arrive at a time when sitting outside and drinking a "spritz" is the perfect antidote to working in the garden or getting the yard back into shape. Their affinity for dandelion is a great example of two ingredients coming into their own in the same season.

STRAWBERRY
DANDELION SPRITZ

2 dandelion flowers

Tiny pinch of Maldon sea salt

½ ounce Salers Aperitif

¼ ounce Strawberry Cordial
(page III)

1½ ounces Aperol

Splash of soda water
(preferably Topo Chico)

Sparkling wine, for topping

Fresh strawberries and parsley,
for garnish

Place the dandelion flowers in a large wine glass and sprinkle a tiny amount of Maldon salt on them. Add the Salers and Strawberry Cordial and very lightly muddle the mixture together. Add the Aperol and fill the glass ¾ full with ice, essentially trapping the dandelions under the ice. Add the splash of soda and a generous amount of sparkling wine (a prosecco would be a fine choice here), and stir the mixture a few times with the straw you'll be drinking out of. Garnish with fresh halved strawberries resting on the rim of the glass and a sprig of parsley.

BOOZING AND INFUSING, GIN & TONIC STYLE

If there's one motto to take away from the Garden-to-Glass ethos, it's "Infuse as You Booze." Just as the Strawberry Dandelion Spritz on page 112 is infused with dandelions right in the glass, any garnish can be used to add complexity to a drink as you or your guests enjoy it, as long as it's actually in the drink and not resting on the glass. All it takes is one leaf of an aromatic herb, or one small piece of radish or cucumber, to make a big impact on the flavor of a drink. There is no better or more common application of this technique than the gin and tonic. Spain's drinking culture is properly credited with launching the resurgence of this classic drink, and with the array of gin and tonics being added to menus all over the world, many bartenders have started approaching garnishing and the subtleties of different botanicals with a thoughtfulness heretofore unknown. Simply put, for the gin and tonic, the game and the glass have changed. While the drink used to be offered in any long tall vessel or rocks glass, bartenders are now offering immersive gin and tonics in wide-mouth cider glasses and wine glasses, which offer the guest an opportunity to experience the marriage of gin, tonic, and an array of botanicals that are inserted in the drink for garnish. The trick to a great one is to harmonize all these different ingredients into a choir of cocktail greatness. Let's break down one example to show how you can use the ingredients in this chapter to create a beautiful, Spanish-style gin and tonic.

The first step is usually picking the gin, or as we did earlier, make your own gin infusion (page 101), and if you have a deep pantry, complete with spices and dried herbs, you can start with the gin and look to strong botanicals like star anise to add complexity (and beauty) to the final drink. But sometimes you have to start with the ingredients you want to feature and find a gin that works best

EUROPEAN
SUMMER G & T

1½ ounces Bristow Gin

3 lemon balm leaves

3 lemon verbena leaves

1 sprig of lemon thyme

2 blackberries, whole

1 strawberry, cut in half, top left on

Q Tonic, to top

Fill a large wine glass, cider glass, or other wide-mouth vessel with ice. Add the gin, herbs, and berries and lightly stir with a long spoon to incorporate the ingredients and begin the "infusion you're about to be boozin'." Gently pour the tonic across the long spoon and into the drink. This is a technique used by many Spanish bartenders at notable gin and tonic bars to keep the bubbles from dissipating too fast as you imbibe. Serve with a straw or a spoon to allow yourself or the guest the opportunity to stir and further incorporate the botanicals, or to steal a berry or two as they drink.

with those ingredients. Here's a list of the key botanicals in some popular gins, which will assist you in choosing the right variety for your gin and tonics, as well as other deliciously aromatic cocktails:

* Bristow — Lemon Verbena

* Beefeater—Oranges

* Plymouth Navy Strength—Angelica

* Tanqueray—Coriander

* Tanqueray No. TEN—Chamomile

* St. George Terroir—Sage and Bay Laurel

* St. George Botanivore—Hops and Black Pepper

* St. George Rye Gin—Lime and Grapefruit Peels

* Corsair Gin—Orris Root and Cucumber

* Sipsmith Gin—Cinnamon and Licorice

* Big Gin—Vanilla and Mint

* Citadelle—Almond and Violet

* Hayman's Old Tom—Lemon Peel and Nutmeg

* The Botanist—Apple Mint and Birch

* Hendricks—Elderflower and Grains of Paradise

Since we're talking berries and lemon herbs here, we're going to look for a gin that goes well with citrus and has bright, herbaceous notes to complement what's growing in the garden. For a gin with bright, peppery, citrus notes, it's hard to beat Bristow Gin from Cathead distillery in Mississippi. We'll also want a mild tonic to allow all these fresh, summery flavors to shine through.

It would be easy to take such a complex and delicious beverage and up the gin amount in order to, you know, turn up the party as well. But that's simply not the point of the Spanish-style gin and tonic. As bartending legend Craig Schoen, the owner and operator of Peninsula, one of Nashville's finest restaurants, hilariously put it, "If the Spaniards were putting 2 or 3 ounces of gin into these drinks they'd have to do even more cocaine than they already do. You want to drink a gin and tonic to putter away the afternoon or evening, getting ready for dinner, which will bring wine and sherry to the table. It's meant to be just a part of the whole evening." Schoen also makes the point that too much gin will overwhelm the subtleties of the aromatics in the garnish and the taste of a good tonic water. He has developed his own tonic, aptly named Peninsula Tonic, which is dry, exquisite, and minimalist, perfect for a "garden G & T." I highly recommend you seek it out.

When I think about all the flavors of summer and how they can be used in drinks, one that I always return to is the ever-spreading, ever-gobbling-up whatever plant surrounds it—the mighty mint. For Chopper, the tiki bar with a robot sci-fi backstory that as of writing this, I'm days away from opening, I'm growing up to eleven different kinds of mint. This will give me plenty of different options to match tasting notes of different rums and classic tiki drinks with different mint varieties like chocolate mint in a Zombie, grapefruit mint to garnish a Hemingway daiquiri, and so on. The other reason I'm growing all of this mint is that it's very easy to grow and take care of. Next up we look at the wide world of mint, along with the most refreshing drink I ever had.

CHAPTER

6

CAFÉ MOJITOS, MINT, & THE SOUL OF CUBA

T urning my bike down a hot, cratered, sunbaked road that seemed like it had been paved in the 1950s, I started back toward Trinidad, Cuba, a colorful, musically vibrant town with cobblestone streets and majestic colonial architecture. I had spent the day riding a rickety cruiser bike out to the beach, a much longer ride than I imagined, passing decades-old billboards with tattered messages like "Socialism or Death," en route to a quiet little beach town called La Boca nestled along the Caribbean Sea. When I returned to Trinidad that evening I would have one of the best drinks of my life, but it was my lunch that day in La Boca that still stands out in my memory. Since I was on a tight budget with no access to an ATM and unable to use any credit card (this was 2009 and spending US dollars was not possible), my lunches were to be as simple as possible. A ham and cheese sandwich for a dollar here and there would leave me with enough cash to explore the music scene and the bars at night.

On my way back through La Boca I passed a little shack with a sign that read "Pizza, 50 cents" in red ink on a piece of rectangular cardboard that was somehow in the shape of the state of Tennessee. There were two tanned, wrinkly gentlemen manning the shack, and though it was a simple setup at best, they did have an enviable view of the sea, bordered by blooming mimosa trees and a bobbing palm tree that moved like a boxer dodging a left hook. I politely asked for a piece in my best high school Spanish and set a 50-cent piece on the splintered red countertop, and since I saw no actual pizza anywhere in sight—no display case, and certainly no pizza oven—I was curious to see how this might unfold. Turning to his left, the man who *wasn't* leaning back on the shack while sitting on three stacked wooden crates and gazing at me with a look that said, "Who is this gringo and what's he doing on that bike?"—in other words, the pizza chef himself—turned to pull off a section from the large piece of dough that I suddenly noticed under the counter. He tossed it into a small metal trash can that was turned sideways to act as a barrel-smoker-oven of sorts, with charcoal burning at the bottom and a small grate sitting just above the charcoal. Here comes the brushing of tomato sauce, I thought, maybe a sprinkling of cheese over the top of this mystery dough that was now baking like my bike tires in the Cuban sun. With a pair of tongs he reached in his sidewalk oven for the baked dough and flung it on a paper plate. Finishing it off with equal squirts from ketchup and mustard bottles, he handed me the pie with a quick downward nod.

We were all sweating profusely. When I asked if he had any beer, he flashed me a sly smile and shook his head no slowly. I imagined he was thinking, *if I did I'd have one in my hand, dipshit.* Since the pie was too hot to scarf down immediately, I sat down on the sidewalk next to my bike and looked out over the water, unsure of which direction I was looking in. I folded the misshapen pie into an imperfect taco of sorts and ate it quickly, glancing back at the men and raising the pie taco up swiftly like a trophy in a classically awkward tourist moment set in a country full of mystery. They stared back blankly at first, but just before I turned around to stare back at the sea, the "pizzaiolo" nodded at me in a brief acknowledgement that was equal parts "I see you" and "just keep eating." As I got up and turned my bike to leave, I luckily had the realization that I needed to take a photo to remember this bizarre lunch encounter at a pizza shack in a small town by the Caribbean Sea. I asked if I could take a photo of their setup and they both nodded slowly. As I took my digital camera out, I noticed the pizzaiolo had his right hand down to his side, cocked into a middle finger like a gun in a holster, ready to bird bomb my touristic intrusion. I took a few photographs, he flashed a quick middle finger and a sly grin, and I was on my way. I turned back up the hills to the glorious city of Trinidad with a lump of dough in my stomach, and a thirst so intense it felt as though I could *smell* water.

Back near the colonial town square of Trinidad, up a large set of cobblestone stairs, music was reverberating off the walls of the nearly 500-year-old town. A passionate *trovador,* Cuba's version of the traveling troubadour, was belting out songs from a platform situated near the top of the steps, accompanying himself on a stout, nylon-stringed guitar. A bar was perched at the top of the stairs with an expansive view of neighboring towns and, once again, the Caribbean Sea, now much farther away and suddenly bathed in the golden light of an oncoming sunset. The bartender, an older mustachioed gentleman with a face like a leather jacket, was dressed in a pressed white shirt and a dark vest and moved like a professional, with economy, speed, and skill. I ordered a mojito (everyone else in the plaza already seemed to have one in their hands) and took note of how he proceeded to make this drink I'd waited for and dreamed about all day.

He dropped a handful of fresh mint and a few spoonfuls of sugar into the glass I'd be drinking out of. The sugar in Cuba is grown on the island, and as with the rum and tobacco that are grown and processed in Cuba, it seems to have a delicious quality all its own. Its equivalent in the United States would be the khaki-colored organic sugar, which differs from light brown or Sugar in the Raw varieties (Florida Crystals is one brand). After adding the mint and the sugar, the bartender took a small hand-held juicer and squeezed what was probably around an ounce of lime juice into my glass. Squeezing the juice directly into the glass retains all the delicious oils and flavor from the lime peel, so you have this interaction between oils and juice as it falls into the glass (at home I would strain the juice as it went into the glass). The bartender then took his weathered wooden muddler, which looked like a miniature baseball bat left out in the rain, and muddled together the mixture of mint, sugar, and lime juice in quick fashion. He didn't use a lot of elbow grease in his technique, he just pressed the ingredients together quickly and efficiently before filling the

CUBAN CAFÉ MOJITO

8 to 10 mint leaves, pulled from the stem,
plus 3 sprigs of mint for garnish

2 scant tablespoons organic sugar

Juice of 1 lime

1 hesitant, very light dash of Angostura bitters

2 to 3 ounces light rum
(preferably Cuban, Dominican,
or Puerto Rican)

1 ounce soda water, or more to taste

Combine the mint and sugar in a large Collins or pint glass. Squeeze the lime juice through a strainer into the glass, and add the bitters. Muddle the ingredients together lightly, being careful not to crush the mint into smithereens. Fill the glass about three quarters full of ice and add the rum. Add the soda and stir the drink briskly with a spoon. Top with a little more soda if desired and a touch more ice. Take 3 sprigs of mint and dust the glass all over with it, grasping the mint stems at the bottom while expressing the oils onto the outside of the glass and into the drink. Place the mint in the drink for garnish, and mojito the day away.

glass three-quarters full with ice. He generously free-poured what seemed like at least three ounces of Havana Club three-year rum (put on Earth to make mojitos with) into the glass and topped it off with a little club soda. Taking a long spoon and stirring the drink briskly, he added another little touch of club soda to finish it off. He then took a few more sprigs of mint and brushed them like a painter across the glass to release the oils, before placing them in the glass for garnish. To my detriment and delight, he served the drink with a straw. I drank it down in about three minutes, long enough for one song from the booming voice of the *trovador.* I sat on the cobblestone steps listening to the singer's beautiful Cuban "country" songs of heartbreak as the sun snuck behind the bay, and wondered what I'd done to be so lucky to be in this place hearing this music and drinking this drink. It was the best drink I had ever had in my young life.

I returned to the seasoned veteran of a bartender for one more mojito, to drink a little more slowly this time, as I budgeted in my head and counted out how many meals I had left on my journey. When all was said and done, after spending eleven days all over the island, I left the country with 40 cents in my pocket. And I loved every minute of it. The people of Cuba are some of the kindest and most creative, gracious, and beautiful souls I have ever met in my travels. I will never forget some of the characters who invited me into their homes for meals, cervezas, and rum—including the now-deceased Cuban guitar master Manuel Galban from the Buena Vista Social Club, but that's another story for another book. I love telling the story of the excitable young man I met in Havana who happened to share my love for basketball, who took me into his home at one in the morning and woke up his wife and three-year-old daughter so I could see his wife *dance.* She was a professional salsa dancer and he felt it was important that I see it up close and have a lesson. To top it off, she wasn't even upset. She threw some music on and shook the floor with her moves, then tried in vain to give me a salsa lesson, all while her bleary-eyed daughter watched in amazement. In their living room. At one in the morning. *That* is the soul of Cuba.

MINT JULEPS AND MORE

Growing mint can be both gratifying and frustrating. Depending on how much space you have and how much you need, mint can take over an entire garden, spreading its tentacles wherever there's dirt until you begin to wonder, "Wait, what else did I even want to plant here?" This can be a positive for beverage professionals and home bar enthusiasts who want to grow their own mint, since it is so ubiquitous as a cocktail garnish. If you're going to be using mint every day in multiple drinks, you're going to need a *lot* of it. So how do you strike that balance of having enough mint without letting it take over other parts of the garden or growing space?

Containers and pots will help to restrict the rhizomes from spreading below the ground and taking over other areas, strangling other plants. And using pots and containers, both free-standing and those that are set into the ground like a plant, is also a great way to experiment with growing different varieties, like pineapple and grapefruit mint, while still keeping a steady supply of everyday mints like Kentucky Colonel or spearmint on hand. Having multiple containers of your everyday mint allows you to switch back and forth between plants when harvesting to allow your mint the time it needs to replenish itself and regenerate. If you need more mint, simply cut a small runner you see starting to spread and plant it somewhere else.

If you have the space, planting different varieties can be a fun way to try different mints with different drinks. Add a pineapple mint garnish to a tiki drink like a Mai Tai to add a tropical layer of aroma and flavor. Or try orange mint in a Paloma to turn an everyday drink

MINT BITTERS

2 cups mint leaves,
pulled from the stem

2 cups mint stems,
cut into 1-inch segments

Zest of 2 limes

3 cardamom pods, cracked

1 teaspoon dried gentian root

1 teaspoon coriander

1 handful of henbit, honeysuckle flowers,
dandelion, or other wildflower (if available)

1 liter 100 proof vodka or pure grain alcohol
(depending on the desired strength)

Combine the mint leaves and stems, lime zest, cardamom, gentian, coriander, and flowers, if using, in a
large mason jar (preferably the 42- or 51-ounce size)
and top with the vodka or grain alcohol. Shake the
mixture vigorously and store in a cool, dark cabinet
away from sunlight. After 2 weeks, strain the mixture
through cheesecloth, squeezing the cloth tightly at the
end to extract as much flavor as possible. Then strain
the mixture through a coffee filter, bottle, and use
within a year, while storing them in a dark cabinet.
One of the more gratifying things about making your
own is that you can experiment with the strength to
suit your tastes: If your bitters are *so* bitter as to be
too strong, simply add a spoonful at a time of a rich
simple syrup (2 parts sugar to 1 part water) until you
taste the astringency fade a little.

into an intoxicating experience as you let the mint infuse into the drink ("infuse as you booze" is our motto), playing off the herbaceous quality of the tequila.

So, how much mint should you plant? It all depends on how much you will need for your culinary and beverage purposes. Providing mint for an entire spring, summer, and fall's worth of drinks for a restaurant or bar drink program? You may want as much as 1 to 2 square yards of mint, or 9 to 18 square feet. If you're just growing mint for the occasional julep and mojito, a few medium-sized pots should do the trick. Mint likes mostly full sun but can handle part shade, depending on your growing zone. Of the 11 zones in the United States, mint can grow in 8 or 9 of them.

Maintaining mint is relatively easy as the more you cut it back, the more vigorous it can become. Having multiple plants going in various spots in your garden will help you manage this more effectively. It will grow as tall as one to two feet if left uncut, with flowers ranging from white to violet to sky blue. Staggering the planting of your mint (starting a few plants in April, and a few more in late May) will allow it to grow and mature at different times, giving you the flexibility to use different parts of the plant to suit your needs. You may want the young leaves to use in a salad with peas, or the flowers for garnishing drinks or making a floral tea blend. The stems can be a great addition to bitters recipes, as they have a refreshing bitter quality when the plants are still young. Here's a simple Mint Bitters recipe (see page 127) that can be a great accompaniment to many of the classic and contemporary cocktails that use mint, either as a garnish or an ingredient. Commercially made bitters just don't have the complexity, freshness, or vibrancy that homemade, straight-from-the-garden bitters will.

The most iconic use for mint is the classic mint julep. Whether you're wearing a silly hat at a Kentucky Derby party or it's just an unbearably hot summer afternoon, the mint julep is many things: tradition and Southern hospitality in a glass, air conditioning in beverage form, an adult snow-cone masquerading as a fancy cocktail, and, with the right preparation, the *easiest* and most fun drink to serve at a party. While it can be a frustrating request for a bartender in the middle of a busy shift (shit, now I have to crush ice, find some decent mint, use up the rest of the mint I had prepped for garnish, and get ready for all the other mint julep orders that are about to come as soon as people see this julep I'm about to make—fuck it! We're out of juleps!), the reason people still want mint juleps, one of the original "fancy" cocktails, is because when executed correctly, it's hard to find a more delicious beverage on planet Earth. Not a bourbon person? Try a julep with any other spirit and maybe a touch of lime juice, and you'll be drinking juleps like some scalawag in a back-alley speakeasy in 1868, stumbling all over the sidewalk on your way home. Don't say I didn't warn you.

One of the keys to a great mint julep, and often a stumbling point at bars that only have the thick "Kold Draft"-style ice cubes, is the ice itself. It should be crushed ice or pellet ice, so if you live near a Sonic Drive-Thru, your problem is solved (I can't believe I'm serious either). You can just head over there, purchase a few large cups of ice, and grab a few tater tots while you're at it. Some Sonics even sell their pellet ice by the bag. If you have a blender you can crush the ice in, that can work too; just be careful to do it in batches of a cup at a time to get a more uniform result. If crushed ice drinks are truly your favorite way to drink cocktails, God bless you, and I suggest a small ice crusher, which can be found online for anywhere from $45 to $90. The crushed ice in a mint julep is crucial as it contributes soothing dilution and bone-chilling frigidity to a drink that is essentially *lots* of bourbon, with a few other things, surrounded by a jungle of fresh mint planted atop a gentle knoll of ice. I love the old illustrations of mid-1800s juleps adorned with so much mint on top that to imbibe one you'd have to sneak your nose

CHOCOLATE MINT JULEP

10 chocolate mint leaves, pulled from the stems

1 tablespoon of superfine sugar
(caster sugar)

1 to 2 dashes of Angostura bitters

1 to 2 dashes of Mint Bitters
(page 127), plus more for garnish

1 teaspoon Nardini Amaro

A very tiny pinch of kosher salt (6 to 8 grains)

3 ounces Kentucky bourbon
(under 100 proof, unless you want to wake up
in the mint patch, which is fine)

Up to 5 mint "trees,"
for garnishing like it's 1879

Combine the mint leaves, sugar, bitters, Nardini, and salt in a shaker tin and muddle without stress. Add the bourbon, a generous amount of crushed ice, and a few regular-sized ice cubes and shake until the drink is very cold. Double strain into a julep cup (if you have one) or an old-fashioned glass over crushed ice. Take a handful of mint "trees" and dust the glass with them, shaking the mint over the top of the drink as well. Throw a few drops of your mint bitters on top for even more complex aromas. Garnish the drink with the mint and serve with a straw. One little trick I also like to use is to fill the julep cup half-full with ice, then add 2 or 3 mint leaves before adding the rest of the crushed ice, thus "hiding" some fresh unmuddled mint in the julep cup to add another layer of complexity. That way, as you jostle your drink here and there, you're releasing even more fresh mint oil into the drink. Be careful, this strong cocktail can go down like cold sweet tea on a hot day. Speaking of tea...

through the mint forest to get a sip. With plenty of mint at your disposal, this should be the model for how your mint juleps should look. Mint grows like crazy and can take over an entire garden bed; juleps need a *lot* of mint to be executed correctly—it is the perfect marriage of ingredient and beverage. Let's go over two methods for the mint julep: a recipe for one person using chocolate mint as well as Nardini Amaro to contribute a chocolate-mint flavor, and a large-scale version that utilizes the classic Kentucky Colonel mint to serve an entire party.

While you may have misgivings about forcing your guests to become temporary mixologists, it can be a fun way to get that often-awkward first hour of a party under way. If you need to nudge the process along, go ahead and make a handful of juleps for those lucky and punctual (but not *too* punctual) first guests. After that, they're on their own!

Note: If you're working with a fresh mint plant and cutting the mint the same day you're using it, it should stay upright and at attention in a cup of cold water. But If your mint is looking limp by the afternoon, try this bartender's trick from Peter Vestinos (barmedic.com), now known as the "Vestinos Method." Dunk your mint head down into an ice bath (just ice and water) and let it sit for 20 minutes. Take the mint out, cut it at a bias once more, and set it into a glass or julep cup that is filled with warm water. Using a julep cup will help retain the heat for a longer period of time. It should stay fresh and vibrant for around 8 hours. This is a great way to bring sad mint back to life if you're working in a restaurant or bar where the mint has been purchased ahead of time and was cut a long time ago in a different state. And it can also help the mint to retain all of its essential oils and hydrate the entire surface area of the herb that will be sitting in your drink, ensuring that your mint will smell amazing and look like a beautiful tree, an anchor in a sea of booze.

SWEET TEA JULEP PARTY

This drink is a great way to host a Derby party or summertime soiree without having to hire a bartender or spend all your time in the kitchen muddling mint, crushing ice, or just drinking the bourbon straight so you feel like you're partying too. It may take a little more prep time, but it'll be worth it. This recipe will serve between 12 to 15 guests.

2 gallons fresh-brewed iced tea

1 to 2 large mint plants,
preferably Kentucky Colonel or spearmint, divided

2 cups white sugar (for the syrup)

2 cups water (for the syrup)

1 lime

1 liter bourbon
(which serves 12 to 15 people around 2 juleps)

1 dasher bottle Angostura, mint,
or other aromatic bitters

THE DAY AHEAD:

Lightly brew the iced tea, add a handful of mint, and place it in the fridge to infuse overnight.

To make a cold-process mint syrup, combine the sugar and water over low heat until the sugar is dissolved, then remove from the heat and let cool. Once the syrup is completely cool, stir in the mint leaves (if the mint is added while the syrup is still warm, you will end up with a brown syrup). Let the syrup infuse overnight in the fridge, or for up to 2 days for a stronger mint flavor.

THE MORNING OF:

Pick the mint you will use for garnishing in the morning after the dew has faded. Cut the ends of the stems at a bias and place them in cold water away from sunlight (see Note on page 131).

Strain the mint out of the tea you made the day before. If you'd like a more minty tea, add a fresh bunch of mint to be strained out before the party.

Zest one lime over the mint syrup, then strain the syrup into a bottle or other container.

Prep your crushed ice situation, either by buying bags of crushed ice, crushing big bags of ice with a hammer, or using an ice crusher. You'll need around 6 pounds of crushed ice for 10 to 15 people.

continued →

AT JULEP PARTY TIME:

Right before your guests arrive, strain the mint tea, if necessary, place it in a pitcher or other serving vessel, and add the mint syrup to taste. You can reserve some unsweetened mint tea, if you like, for guests who are "off the sugar." Set the pitcher on the table or counter you're using for your julep-making station.

Set out the mint for garnishing (keeping it in water), the bourbon, and the bitters. Feel free to offer other spirits at the station as well, for guests who may not like bourbon.

Place your crushed ice in a large bowl with a julep strainer, large spoon, or scoop for ladling the ice into cups.

To make each julep at the station: Fill a julep cup or other glass halfway with crushed ice. Add 2 to 3 ounces bourbon, then add 2 dashes of bitters.

Add the mint sweet tea and more crushed ice and lightly stir to incorporate. Top with more ice, garnish with a bouquet of fresh mint, and you're done! Party on.

Mint is a member of the *Labiatae* family of herbs, most of which are native to the Mediterranean. One of the most pleasant aspects of growing herbs from the *Labiatae* family is their appeal to all kinds of butterflies and bees, which bring their pollination magic to anything you grow. It makes mint a great choice for growing in the spring as you're establishing your garden and into the summer as well. And you'll need that pollination army if you're going to grow some vegetables, which we'll tackle next.

CHAPTER

7

DRINK YOUR VEGETABLES, PIMP YOUR PIMM'S,

& Love Your Lovage

With its garden full o' garnish, complete with herbs, vegetables, and berries, there is perhaps no better drink to embody the spirit of Garden-to-Glass drinking than the Pimm's No. 1 Cup. As with so many elixirs whose secret formulas have stood the test of time, Pimm's first iteration was as a health tonic. The original formula, developed by James Pimm, the owner of an oyster bar in a lively area of London, was first concocted in 1823 (200-year anniversary party anyone?) as a means to differentiate his establishment from the numerous bars in the neighborhood and to offer something "healthier" and lighter than gin. It was served in smaller-than-usual tankard vessels (like a small wooden or metal beer stein), giving it the name "No. 1 Cup." Though the base of this curious elixir is gin, it's much lighter than gin, coming in at 25 percent alcohol, and is infused with a kitchen's worth of berries, spices, and proprietary botanicals, including quinine. The cocktail now known simply as the Pimm's Cup has mutated into a sort of sangria on steroids, but has, for most of its life, been a long tall mixture of Pimm's No. 1 and sparkling lemonade, with a garnish bouquet featuring cucumber, mint, green apple, and strawberry. In London it has been the signature drink of Wimbledon for decades, and according to *Wine Enthusiast*, over 80,000 pints of Pimm's Cup are sold during the tournament every year.

In 1940, Pimm's No. 1 migrated to New Orleans and found a spot on the menu of The Napoleon House Bar, where the Pimm's Cup became so popular, a myth began to develop that the drink actually hailed from New Orleans. While this isn't true, the crescent city can lay claim to such classics as the Sazerac, the Brandy Crusta, the Ramos Gin Fizz, and about eight other amazing drinks—oh yeah, and jazz—so it's not like they needed another beautiful creation attributed to their incomparable city. In New Orleans, a Pimm's Cup has come to mean Pimm's with lemon and lime soda, with a touch of ginger beer thrown in to some versions. Since New Orleans was an early torch-bearer of the current cocktail renaissance, there are now many incredible variations on this drink served throughout the city. The drink's revival 10 to 12 years ago led many cocktail masters to try their hand at turning this ultimate summer drink into a fall and winter cocktail, leaning into the spices of Pimm's and bolstering it with flavors like rosemary and thyme. Some would even swap out the sparkling lemonade for more robust brown ales, or would flip the drink on its head and use bitter lemon soda with muddled vegetables like celery. Perhaps the Pimm's Cup's most fun attribute is that it's an idea, a template meant for exploring in large format (it is still frequently served at London garden parties and polo matches in pitcher form), as a tall easy tumbler, or as a refined craft cocktail.

I would tend to agree with the British on this one, as the Pimm's Cup is a perfect punch to serve at a summer soiree. You can batch the punch ahead of time and really put the *garden* in garden party by infusing some botanicals in the punch overnight. This drink is a great exercise in "choose your own adventure" cocktailing, since you can make it as complicated, fussy, and fancy as you like—or not. And since we're talking about a drink that's usually garnished like a whole salad on a pick, it's also a good excuse to put all those obscure herbs you're growing to use. Three herbs we'll dive into in this chapter can take a Pimm's Cup to another level. Borage, with its beautiful blue and white blossoms and cucumber-esque flavor, is a great choice for this drink and any other drink with vegetal, herbaceous tones. Salad Burnet, a shade-tolerating, curious little herb with tasting notes of melon and cucumber, also works very well in a Pimm's Cup. Lovage, a glorious celery-flavored herb with a hollow stem perfect for making straws out of, can give any drink a vegetal aroma boost simply by being the garnish. To best execute this drink as a party-pitcher-porch-pounder (my favorite category of cocktail), you can prep the drink the night before and let the

PIMM'S CUP PUNCH

2 quarts Lemonade

14 ounces Pimm's No. 1

4 ounces Plymouth gin

Juice and hulls of 2 lemons,
plus additional as needed

3 leaves and 8 flowers of borage

5 sprigs of salad burnet

2 sprigs of lovage

3 mint leaves

1 sprig of lemon thyme

3 leaves lemon balm

3 leaves lemon verbena

Blueberries, strawberries,
and/or blackberries, for garnish

Cucumber slices, for garnish

Green apple slices, for garnish

Additional herbs and flowers, for garnish

Soda water, optional

Sparkling wine, optional

THE DAY BEFORE THE PARTY:

Combine the lemonade, Pimm's, gin, and lemon juice and
hulls in a large container.

Cut a large piece of cheesecloth, spread it out, and place the borage, salad burnet, lovage, mint, lemon thyme, lemon balm, and lemon verbena on top. Wrap the herbs in the cheesecloth and tie the top together with a little garden twine. Clap the satchel in your hands a few times to release the oils in the herbs, then place it in the container with the liquid. Stir the batch a few times to further incorporate the herbs, and let sit in the refrigerator overnight.

THE DAY OF THE PARTY:

Cut your garnish sometime in mid-morning, before the day gets too hot and the herbs begin to wilt. Choose whatever herbs, fruits, and vegetables are growing in your garden that inspire you. Dunk herbs like borage, lovage, salad burnet, mint, and lemon verbena in cold water until party time. Store blossoms like borage flowers and honeysuckle in an airtight container in the refrigerator. Prepare berries in advance by placing one of each berry on a cocktail pick. Before the guests arrive, set up the "garnish garden" next to where the punch will be served, arranging the herbs in different cups with labels. When you're ready to set the punch out, remove the bouquet garni (see page 145) and lemon hulls from the punch and taste it. Adjust the sweetness or acidity of the punch as you see fit, either by adding a little more lemon juice or adding some sugar. If you'd like to add some bubbles to your Pimm's Cup Punch you can add soda water, or, to make it a "Pimm's Cup Royale," add some sparkling wine. Add your forest of herbs, some berries on a pick, and a cucumber or apple slice and there you have it, summer in a glass.

THE ULTIMATE PIMM'S CUP

½ ounce Parsley Cordial (recipe page 150)

1 strawberry, halved, tops left on, divided

One slice of cucumber, quartered,
plus 1 long peeled slice for garnish

2 sprigs of salad burnet

2 borage leaves

Tiny pinch of Maldon sea salt

½ ounce fresh lemon juice

¼ ounce fresh lime juice

1½ ounces Pimm's No. 1

¾ ounce botanical-forward gin
(like The Botanist, St. George Botanivore,
or Citadelle)

Soda water (preferably Topo Chico)

Mint leaves, salad burnet leaves,
and/or borage flowers, for garnish

Combine the parsley cordial, one half of the strawberry, the cucumber, salad burnet, borage, and salt in a shaker tin. Muddle the ingredients together, using enough pressure to break up the cucumber. Add the lemon and lime juice, then pour the Pimm's and gin over your muddler and into the tin to "wash" off any ingredients stuck to the muddler. Fill a Collins glass or tumbler with ice and add a little soda water to the bottom of the glass. Shake all the ingredients until well chilled and double strain the drink into the prepared glass. Give it a stir to incorporate the soda water, then garnish with a long, peeled slice of cucumber inserted in the drink, the other half of the strawberry, and some combination of mint, salad burnet, and borage flowers. While this drink may be a *tad* ingredient-heavy for a bar to serve, this is the kind of all-in drink you can make when you're growing or have access to some of these lovely botanicals. Cucumber juice can be an amazing modifier in this drink as well (I thought it cruel to include in the main recipe, giving you so much prep time). You can alter this recipe by swapping tequila for the gin and celery for the cucumber, or by using bourbon, rhubarb, and raspberries in place of gin and cucumber. This is just a guide for an ultimate Garden-to-Glass experience.

CUCUMBER
BLOSSOM CORDIAL

1 quart organic sugar

1 pint water

1 cucumber

1 pint cucumber blossoms,
picked over the course of 4 to 5 days

Zest of 1 lime

1 teaspoon Maldon sea salt

½ teaspoon citric acid

2 sprigs of fresh dill
or 2 dill flower heads

5 drops rosewater

Combine the sugar and water over low heat, stirring until the sugar is dissolved. Remove from the heat and transfer to the refrigerator to cool. Peel the cucumber, reserving the peels, then chop the cucumber flesh. Once the syrup is cold, add the cucumber and its peels, the freshly picked blossoms, and the lime zest, salt, citric acid, dill, and rosewater. Stir to incorporate and slightly agitate the ingredients, then return to the refrigerator to infuse. Over the course of the next four days, pick more blossoms as they appear and add them to the syrup. Taste and strain when the flavor is strong enough. Bottle and store in the refrigerator. The cordial will keep for about a month.

ingredients infuse in the refrigerator, then set up a garnish station the day of the party, letting guests add their own twist to the drink. Using a "bouquet garni," a French cooking technique traditionally used to add herbal punch to sauces, marinades, and braises, you can easily add complex herbal flavors to your cocktails overnight. The bouquet garni is nothing more than herbs wrapped in cheese-cloth and tied together so that you can easily pull the bouquet out of whatever it's infusing into. This punch will serve between 8 to 10 people.

In addition to being an ideal porch-pounding party sensation, the Pimm's Cup is a great drink template for an intricate craft cocktail, utilizing a mountain of garden herbs, wild botanicals, and in-season vegetables. It's also a great drink to begin easing the mighty fresh cucumber into your drinking arsenal. Cucumber pairs well with gin and tequila but can also add some refreshing, cooling flavors to a vodka or pisco drink. It can be muddled, juiced, or peeled thinly and placed in a drink as part of the garnish, which will release its fresh flavor as you drink the cocktail (infuse as you booze, baby!), turning a drink into a journey that tastes different by the time you finish it. For this version of a Pimm's Cup, we'll both muddle and peel a strip of cucumber to get plenty of that refreshing summer flavor. The recipe also makes use of borage, which is ideal as a muddling botanical because the leaves are thick and juicy, and can be too rough for salads.

CUCUMBER COOLER

2 ounces cucumber juice

1 ounce Cucumber Blossom Cordial (page 144)

½ ounce lime juice

½ ounce lemon juice

2 drops rosewater

3 mint leaves
(or try salad burnet or borage,
if you have them), plus more for garnish

Tiny pinch of salt

Soda water
(preferably Topo Chico)

Borage flowers, for garnish

Combine the cucumber juice, cordial, lime juice, lemon juice, rosewater, mint, and salt in a Collins glass or tumbler and stir to incorporate. Add ice and soda water and garnish with mint and borage flowers. This drink also works well shaken and served up like a martini; garnish with a slice of cucumber and some borage flowers on top of the slice, floating like a lily pad.

RAISING A TOAST TO VEGETABLES

One of the quandaries for me when I think about growing cucumber is: do I actually need to? I have access to fresh cucumbers; during the summer, they're plentiful at markets and roadside stands near my home in Nashville. And a cucumber plant can take up quite a bit of space in the garden, crawling over and around anything it can get its hands on and strangling nearby plants with its outstretched arms. Depending on how many cucumbers you plan on using and how much space you have, this abundance can be a good or a bad thing. But one year, my cucumbers totally took off, so I trellised them and allowed them to climb and move freely, adding another trellis along the way. That summer I discovered an amazing ingredient I hadn't had the opportunity to use much, as they are almost never sold in markets: cucumber blossoms. These gold flowers of wonder can add so much to a simple salad, a cordial, a bitters recipe, or even a limeade. They taste and smell exactly like you would imagine, with a note of rose petal, making them ideal for any number of infusions and a lovely ingredient to have around in the summer. Just remember that if you use as many flowers as you can, you won't have many actual cucumbers to pick. When the flowers are picked fresh in mid-morning (lightly pinch them off the stalk) and used that same day, they add an element that is nearly impossible to find outside of your own garden. Here's my recipe for Cucumber Blossom Cordial (see page 144), using a four-day process where you add more cucumber blossoms each day, at the peak of their season. This can be shortened to a one-day process, but the flavor and aroma will be incredible if you stretch out the process and add more blossoms along the way.

Whether you're a professional bartender or a home enthusiast, you know the need for a tasty nonalcoholic drink that also pairs well with food. The Cucumber Blossom Cordial is a great tool for sophisticated nonalcoholic beverages, and is amazing when used with

CELERY BITTERS

4 to 5 large stalks of the freshest
celery possible, leaves and all,
washed under cold water, chopped

½ cup fresh lovage, chopped

Zest of 1 lemon

1 sprig of thyme

1 tablespoon celery seeds

½ teaspoon dried gentian root

28-30 ounces vodka

Celery Cordial (recipe follows), to taste

THREE WEEKS AHEAD:

Combine the celery, lovage, lemon zest, thyme, celery seeds, and
gentian root in a 32-ounce Mason jar and top with the vodka.
Seal the jar, shake it like it's going out of style, and store the
jar in a cool, dark place to let the botanicals infuse for 2 weeks.
Shake the mixture every other day to agitate the ingredients and
release more flavor into the bitters.

ONE WEEK AHEAD:

Taste the mixture and, if you'd like a stronger celery flavor, chop
more celery or lovage and add it to the batch. Let the bitters
steep for another week. If you don't already have Celery Cordial
on hand, prepare it now.

WHEN READY TO USE:

Strain the ingredients through cheesecloth, squeezing the cloth to
extract as much flavor as possible. To increase the celery flavor
and decrease the astringency of the bitters, add the celery cordial
1 tablespoon at a time to your bitters mixture until you have a
nice, clean, dry bitterness. Keep the remaining celery cordial to
use in a batch of Bloody Mary mix (page 155).

PARSLEY CORDIAL

I cup parsley leaves and stems, chopped
2 cups white sugar
I cup water
zest of I lemon

I cup tightly packed parsley leaves and stems, chopped up and infused into a chilled rich syrup of 2 cups white sugar, I cup water, and zest of one lemon. Infuse for I to 2 days, strain, bottle, and store in the refrigerator.

CELERY CORDIAL

4 cups organic sugar
2 cups water
2 cups chopped celery stalks

Combine the sugar and water over low heat, stirring to dissolve. Add the celery and simmer for 20 minutes, then remove from the heat and place in the refrigerator to infuse overnight. Taste and strain when the syrup is flavored to your liking. Bottled and stored in the refrigerator, the cordial will keep for a month.

cucumber juice. This drink pairs well with oysters, salads, and light starters, and even provides a cooling counterpart to fried chicken.

Another vegetable that's ideal in cocktails, whether juiced, muddled, or as a garnish, is celery. Celery is a backbone aromatic in the world of cooking, part of the "holy trinity" in Cajun and New Orleans-style cooking (celery, onions, bell peppers) and part of the essential "mirepoix" of French cooking (two parts onion to one part celery and one part carrot). Celery's starring role as a cocktail ingredient is usually the Bloody Mary, where stalks are used much like swizzle sticks to stir the drink and release even more vegetal flavor. But I've always enjoyed celery with blanco tequila, vegetal Italian amaros like Cynar (made with artichokes) and Sfumato Rabarbaro, a smoked rhubarb amaro practically put on this Earth to be used in mezcal and tequila drinks. Celery isn't new to the beverage game: It has been used in Chinese medicine for centuries, and surged in popularity toward the end of the nineteenth century in America, where it was used in "celery tonics" meant to cure digestive woes and was touted as a superfood. We've come full circle now, as celery juice had a moment in the news cycle as recently as February 2019, with Morweena Ferrior of The Guardian writing, "Anyone who's anyone is juicing celery at the moment," and noting that celery sales had increased by 454 percent. Somebody pass me the tequila!

Dr. Brown, namesake of the famous soda company from New York City, debuted his carbonated Celery Tonic in 1868, eventually changing the name to "Cel-Ray Soda." Though the company has changed hands a few times over the decades, Cel-Ray is still produced and has an incomparable vegetal, citrus, and pepper backbone, making it an obvious choice to use in any gin, tequila, vodka, or mezcal highball or craft cocktail. Especially when garnished with lovage, a celery-flavored herb from the parsley family that will snatch your heart once you experience its celery-packed

LOVE JUAN COLLINS

2 sprigs of lovage,
tops cut from the stems and reserved for garnish,
stems chopped into 2-inch segments
(if lovage is not available,
substitute celery stalks and tops)

¼ ounce Sfumato Rhubarb Amaro

Pinch of Maldon sea salt

Dr. Brown's Cel-Ray Soda

2 ounces blanco tequila

½ ounce lime juice

¼ ounce grapefruit juice

Combine the lovage stems, amaro, and salt in a shaker tin and muddle to release the lovage flavor. Fill a Collins glass or tumbler with ice and add an inch or two of the Cel-Ray soda to the bottom of the glass. Add the tequila, lime juice, and grapefruit juice to the shaker tin, and shake vigorously. Strain the drink over the Cel-Ray soda, top with a little more soda, and garnish with the lovage tops. You can also use another sprig of lovage, with its hollow stem, as a straw for a completely immersive drinking experience, which is always recommended! Feeling healthy yet?

aroma, anything made with Cel-Rey Soda will be unique and delicious, and may even trick you into thinking a tequila and soda can actually be healthy.

If you like gardening challenges and testing your patience, growing celery can humble you as a home gardener. You'll gaze off into the distance toward the nearest grocery store or farmer's market and think to yourself, "It's for sale right over there; what am I doing trying to grow this shit? It's not even doing anything!" However, there is one heirloom varietal known as "Tall Utah" with amazing flavor that, with a little patience, is relatively easy to grow and will yield plenty of tasty, aromatic stalks. It may take a year or so to get a sizable root, but the stalks and leaves of Tall Utah celery have so much beautiful celery flavor, you won't believe the difference between home-grown and store bought. I've talked to a lot of chefs about ingredients that shine when they come straight from a garden or a local farm, and many of them mention celery as a standout. Freshly plucked and locally grown celery can be hard to find, which is all the more reason to try growing it yourself. You can take the tops and leaves and make a celery bitters with them to enjoy that flavor for months.

To grow Tall Utah celery you'll need to set aside some space in a cool, less-well-drained area of your garden with plenty of organic matter mixed in, as celery enjoys cool and wet conditions. Seedlings should be started indoors 9 to 12 weeks before being planted outside. They can be planted outdoors 2 weeks before the last spring frost, and should be spaced out by around 8 inches per plant. If you're planting rows, space them 2 to 3 feet apart. Tall Utah is a biennial plant, meaning you'll get around two years out of one plant. You can harvest the stalks and leaves after 100 days (or less if you want to pick them young), but may need to wait until the following year to harvest the root and all. When freshly harvested, celery can have a mild bitterness, which will fade over a few days in the refrigerator. For our purposes, we'll harness that bitterness to make cocktails all year long.

Lovage is important to recognize when working with celery since growing celery can be difficult and requires a bit of space that you may want to save for, you guessed it, lovage. For those with limited space or the patience for celery, lovage is an ideal substitute. This hollow-stemmed herb can require some patience to start, but it's quite hardy and will last until Thanksgiving in most climates, when I always reach for it to use in stuffing, cornbread, carrot dishes, and yes, drinks! Lovage can be started in pots or starters indoors five to six weeks before the last frost. The seedlings require a good bit of water, though they offer a lesson in garden planning and soil management due to their insistence on well-drained soil. If you're starting your first garden and you have a patch of dirt that seems sandy, rocky, or just plain head-scratchingly dry, this would be a perfect spot for lovage. If you're using raised beds, pots, or containers, you'll want to take care not to over-water your lovage, and to give it plenty of space to stretch its wings. Lovage can grow up to six or seven feet tall, but you'll love it so much in your daily arsenal for eggs, sandwiches, and salads, it probably won't reach that height. A trick you can use for cocktails is to muddle or shake the stems into drinks, which will release a pleasant celery flavor and also be very easy to strain, keeping any crushed, tiny bits of green out of the drink. Then you can use the tops in the drink as a garnish, which will add a lifting, vegetal aroma and bolster the lovage flavor as well. Try this method in this tequila cooler (see page 152), an herbaceous take on a Tom Collins.

GARDEN TO GLASS BLOODY MARY MIX

2 quarts tomato juice

12 ounces celery juice

6 ounces beet juice

3 ounces cucumber juice

3 ounces lemon juice

1 ounce lime juice

3 ounces Celery Cordial (page 150)

2 ounces pickle juice
(juice from any type of pickle liquid will do)

6 dashes Celery Bitters (page 149)

3 tablespoons kosher salt

12 turns freshly ground black pepper

2 tablespoons prepared horseradish

2 tablespoons celery seed

2 tablespoons dried dill
(or dill weed, but I don't know why it's called a weed
just because it's dried)

1 tablespoon onion powder

2 teaspoons basil seed

2 teaspoons celery salt

2 teaspoons paprika
(smoked paprika if you've got it)

Pinch of dried marjoram

1 teaspoon garlic powder

25 to 50 dashes hot sauce
(like Valentina)

A few shakes of dried cayenne pepper

continued →

Combine all the ingredients *except* the hot sauce and cayenne in a large sterilized container and whisk vigorously to incorporate. If you have a stick blender, that will do wonders in terms of mixing everything together. Taste the mix and add hot sauce to taste, depending on how hot you like your Bloody Mary; then add the cayenne. This will give the mix a lot of "pop," so add a little at a time until you're happy with the flavor. Kept in the refrigerator, the mix will last for around 2 weeks.

THE BLOODY MARY—
FOR BETTER OR WORSE

The bloody mary is the ubiquitous vegetable cocktail. It has evolved from a simple can't-screw-this-up concoction to increasingly ornate presentations featuring a cornucopia of ingredients. Alas, not always for the best.

I have a difficult relationship with the Bloody Mary cocktail. While it's certainly one of the most popular drinks around, crushed on brunchy weekends like cans of beer at a frat party, I have never been a fan of the drink. And don't get me started on the garnishes, which have gone so far in recent years as to include fried chicken, eggs, and even cans of beer, to which I must firmly plant my flag on the mountain of NO. No, I would not put a goddamn chicken dinner in a Bloody Mary the size of a water jug, and guess what, I prefer the eggs and bacon on my plate at brunch time. I don't want a skewered biscuit sitting on a beer stein of Bloody Mary; I want my biscuit doused in country gravy and on my plate, giving the acidic peppery bomb of a Bloody Mary something to sit on top of.

Of course, I have some bias, maybe even a reason to loathe the Bloody Mary. I've made so much Bloody Mary mix at various bartending jobs over the years (we went through around 24 quarts every 10 days at Husk!) that the mere smell of tomato juice makes me feel a surge of panic that all the Bloody Mary mix is going to run out. With all that said, I am a professional, and when made with love and fresh ingredients, a good Bloody Mary can truly lift the spirit. And I firmly believe that a good celery and lovage garnish can bring the Bloody Mary back down to earth where it belongs, instead of an afterthought under some towering garnish that is most likely going to be thrown in the trash. I also believe the reason the Bloody Mary exists is to cure a hangover, and to do that you'll need some heat, celery, and beet juice, and a good mix of salt, sweet, acid, and spices. This recipe serves six of your hungover friends (see page 155).

Another Bloody Mary "hack" I can offer is to use the bouquet garni technique to infuse the batch overnight with an assortment of chopped root vegetables, especially turnips, which go amazingly well with a Bloody Mary's peppery bite. Lay a large piece of cheesecloth out and place chopped parsnips, carrots, turnips, celery, and thyme in the center. Wrap them up and tie the bouquet together, then place in the Bloody Mary mix to infuse overnight. Remove the bouquet the next day, saving the vegetables to cook in a "bloody marinated" hash, and promptly have your mind blown.

And about that garnish: Since we're singing the praises of all our herbal friends in this book, I encourage you to add any number of herbs in harmony with your Bloody Mary mix. Lovage and celery are both obvious choices and can be lovely counterpoints to the celery in the mixture. Parsley, marjoram, onion, garlic scapes, thyme, rosemary, and sage are all great choices. While I'm personally not crazy about meat being included, a small piece of cured ham can be a fun little tease before a big brunch. And pickles on a pick are also a great way to offer the imbiber a little bite of flavor to offset the liquid-lunch quality of the drink. But I beg you, please, no fried chicken or biscuits. Keep the fried food on the plate.

One last trick of the trade I can offer on using vegetable juice in cocktails, Bloody Mary mixes, or garden punches is to use citric acid and malic acid (which hilariously and accurately auto-corrects as "magic acid"). While all fruit and vegetables contain citric acid, some juices, like beet and carrot, can be sweeter than you may realize. Depending on the flavor you're looking for in the drink you're making, citric and malic acids, along with salt, can help to decrease your reliance on lemon or lime juice, which can overwhelm the subtleties in the subtleties in fresh vegetable juice cocktails or nonalcoholic drinks. One basic formula would be to add ¼ teaspoon citric acid for every pint of carrot juice to increase the acidity and tame the sweetness. This will also add some shelf life to the juice. However, most vegetable juices will only keep for 48 hours and are best used within 12 hours after the vegetable has been juiced. Malic acid is the tart acid found in apples, pears, grapes, and rhubarb and can broaden the flavor of beet juice when added in a ratio of ¼ teaspoon per pint of beet juice. If you'll be using a cordial or syrup in a cocktail you're making with vegetable juice, add a pinch of salt to the drink to tame the sweetness of the juice interacting with the syrup. Experimenting with acids can open up a whole new world of flavor manipulation and could be the topic of a whole new book. Just be careful as acids are corrosive, and always wear gloves when handling them.

Now that we've covered what *not* to do when garnishing a drink, let's further explore the principles of good garnishing and creating a more immersive experience with a cocktail.

CHAPTER

8

STEPPING UP *the* GARNISH GAME

So much of the Garden-to-Glass ethos lies in the ability to use easy-to-grow herbs to transform the way you drink. Where this idea really shines is in the execution of the garnish. One of the first times I began to focus on the garnish as an immersive experience in both aroma and flavor was in the walk-in cooler at Husk. It was a busy lunch shift and in so many ways, I had run out of thyme. I began the brisk walk from the bar to the walk-in, which was located in the backyard of the Antebellum mansion on Rutledge Hill in Nashville. On my hunt for thyme for an iced tea cocktail, I happened to run into our Chef de Cuisine Brian Baxter, who was in the walk-in checking orders and dreaming up new dishes.

"You have a second?" he said as I grabbed a handful of fresh thyme from an herb drawer. From one inquisitive mind to the other, the answer to Chef Baxter was always, "yup."

"Try this," he said, handing me a rather large purple dinosaur leaf that was wrapped around a blueberry. I immediately smelled basil, baking spices, and the light summery flavor of the blueberry. "Shiso and blueberry," he confirmed. "Try it."

I popped the little bite in my mouth and was amazed at the variety of flavors. It was like eating a slice of blueberry pie with an herb crust. I immediately wondered, *how can I make this into a drink?* Spices, herbs, blueberries, summer flavors…. But then I realized that it would also be special to share the experience of biting into the shiso-blueberry combination as part of a drinking experience. So I combined both ideas into one drink, the Shiso Caipirinha with blueberries.

Shiso is one of the ideal Garden-to-Glass ingredients, as it's easy to grow in most growing zones in the United States and it grows rapidly in the wild. Its spiced, basil-like aroma and mint-esque propensity to take over any area it grows makes it an easy herb to count on throughout the summer months and into early fall, when the tiny hot pink flowers come out spraying color all over the garden. Not to get too Jimi Hendrix on you, but it smells like what the color purple would smell like. Try it, let me know. Later in the summer, purple shiso shows off little fireworks of pink flowers which produce a whole new level of shiso-basil-rose quality that works well shaken into drinks or used as garnish.

If wrapping a blueberry in a shiso leaf is not your cup of tea or you're not able to source these fine ingredients at the right time, there are other, easier methods to garnish a drink while making the experience memorable. A good garnish can be as simple as clapping mint into your hands before placing it in the glass, which "wakes up" the essential oils and immediately brings the aroma of the mint to the fore. Or striping your lemon twist with a channel knife *over* the martini so as to release the oils of the citrus over the drinking surface. You may even prefer a flamed orange peel over the glass, both for show, and to impart a subtle smoky flavor in a Manhattan or old fashioned–style drink (use a match when trying this so you don't impart off flavors from the lighter into the glass). These little garnishing details go a long way toward taking a drink from ordinary to elegant and extraordinary. And as with the blueberry-and-shiso combination, thinking about flavor affinities, such as strawberry and rhubarb, or lime and cloves, is a great place to start when creating unique and unforgettable garnishes.

The "lime studded with clove" is a lovely, aromatic garnish common in tiki drinks that offers a fresh equatorial note from the fresh lime and a deep, affecting note from the cloves. This is a perfect garnish for nearly any rum cocktail, whether floated in a coupe for a spiced daiquiri or plopped atop a mountain of crushed ice in a swizzle. If rosemary is easily attainable, you can take this garnish one step further by studding the lime with clove and rosemary to

SHISO-BLUEBERRY CAIPIRINHA

4 blueberries,
plus one more for garnish

4 large shiso leaves,
plus one large leaf for garnish

½ ounce simple syrup,
equal parts water and sugar

¼ ounce Pasubio Amaro
(if you can't find this Amaro,
imported by Haus Alpenz,
try 2 dashes of Angostura bitters
and more blueberries)

1½ ounces Cachaca
(Novo Fogo is a great one)

½ ounce Rhum Agricole
(try Neisson Blanc)

¾ ounce lime juice

In a shaker tin, muddle the blueberries, shiso, syrup,
and amaro together and add the remaining ingredients,
pouring the booze over the muddler so as not to leave
any delicious botanicals stuck to the muddler. Shake
the drink vigorously with plenty of ice and double
strain into a rocks glass over ice. Garnish by sticking
a pick through one end of a shiso leaf, into a blueberry
and then through the other end of the shiso leaf, like
a sail with a blueberry in the middle. To your humble
author, this might be the most dynamic and delicious
drink in this book.

give a "palm tree" effect. The swizzle, the West Indian liquid cool-me-down, is a great vehicle for this garnish and provides the perfect template for all kinds of hot-weather experimentation. For the crushed ice, either go to Sonic for those perfect little pebbles of ice, or you can crush your own in a blender or ice crusher.

THE FIRST FLORAL GARNISHES OF SPRING

Eastern Redbud, a very common tree across all but two growing zones in the United States, is one of the most welcome sights in early spring, when fresh garnishing options can be hard to come by. The trees flash colors of pink, red, and purple in such a rush they often play tricks on the eyes. If you approach one slowly you'll notice that the tiny blossoms are both pink and red, smell slightly of roses, and taste a little like strawberry. While the flavor and aroma of these tiny little blossoms is very light, they make for striking garnishes, in which the blossoms can even be left on parts of a small branch for a more elaborate approach. Combined with other floral spring bounty like forsythia and wisteria, they can contribute to decorative floral arrangements for your home, bar, or restaurant. Since the season for flowering redbud and other springtime new-comers can be quite short, a way to make them last throughout the year is by pickling them in a large jar with white vinegar. You can add spices like allspice, cinnamon, and clove, and use the flowers down the road for decorating drinks and plates of food. Redbud holds up particularly well when pickled. The flowers, fresh or pickled, look amazing sitting on that pillow of white foam created in an egg-white cocktail, where their delicate nature can be experienced by the drinker. To go a step further, you can try spraying a light mist of flower water on the cocktail to play with the sensory effects of the garnish.

SUMMER DAZE SWIZZLE

2 ounces dark Jamaican rum
(preferably Hamilton Black, Smith and Cross,
or Plantation Jamaican Dark)

¾ ounce fresh lime juice

½ ounce Taylor's Velvet Falernum

1 teaspoon St. Elizabeth Allspice Dram

1 dash angostura bitters

1 lime wheel

5 cloves studded in a circle
around the wheel

1 small sprig rosemary

Combine all the ingredients over crushed ice in the glass you'll
be serving the drink in, and "swizzle" with a long spoon or swizzle
stick (available on Amazon and Cocktail Kingdom) by rapidly
spinning the spoon or stick between your palms to chill the drink
and mix the ingredients together. When thoroughly chilled, top
the drink with a little more crushed ice and garnish with the lime
wheel studded with 5 cloves around the wheel and the small
sprig of rosemary pierced through the center of the lime wheel.
Umbrellas are optional. Drink (not too fast!) with a straw. Be
careful using metal straws with extremely cold beverages with
crushed ice, because the straw may become so cold it can stick
to your lips like the flagpole in *A Christmas Story*! Who's thirsty?

OTHER IMMERSIVE, GARDEN-TO-GLASS

GARNISHES

WITH COLORED ILLUSTRATION BY BRIAN BAXTER

Wood sorrel /
strawberry garnish
with parsley

- Celery twist with lovage
  flowers

- Wrapped orange twist
  around thyme with sage
  blossoms

- Nasturtium Lily pad
  with little thyme
  flowers inside the big
  nasturtium flower like a
  cornucopia

Mint cut into three
pieces on fresh or
dehydrated lime garnish

- Romanesco Mount Rushmore in an egg white drink. Herbs plucked into the holes of a piece of Romanesco sitting in an egg white drink like a mountain in the clouds

- A clear block of ice with flowers and thyme inside

- Watercress flowers coming out of the hole of a raspberry

- Large white magnolia flower with nasturtium flower in the middle and purple clover flower inside that

Wrapped lemon twist around rosemary with mint flowers tucked into the spindly rosemary needles

Fanned out apples / cinnamon stick with thyme stuck in the cinnamon stick hole

Peach slice
covered with
elderflowers

- Cracked spices over
  egg white on one
  half of coupe, with
  purple basil flowers
  on top of basil leaf
  on the other

- Smoked paprika rim
  with small lavender
  flowers dotted
  along it

- Cucumber lattice
  with roses coming
  out of the sides in
  a Collins glass

Toasted spices on pear
and rosemary, with the
spices torched as they get
dusted on top of pear

PICKLED REDBUD
(OR OTHER SPRINGTIME)
BLOSSOMS

3 cups redbud blossoms

30 ounces white vinegar

1 teaspoon allspice berries

1 tablespoon whole cloves

1 cinnamon stick, crushed

10 black peppercorns

1 teaspoon superfine sugar

Pinch of salt

Wash the redbud blossoms delicately under cold water and set them aside to dry. Once dry, add them to a 32-ounce Mason jar (add more blossoms if you can fit them), along with the spices, sugar, and salt. Shake the mixture and let it sit at room temperature in a cool, dark cabinet for a month. The blossoms can be used, as long as they're submerged in the vinegar, for up to 4 months.

Whether it's fresh-from-the-garden herbs and flowers, spices cracked over a drink, or fresh fruits and vegetables, with all their multitudes of flavors from peel to stem to leaves, there are so many ingredients to choose from on your path to garnishing gold. But garnishing is not the only way to finish a drink, and sometimes plunging these ingredients into liquid to create a syrup, shrub, tincture, or cordial, can be the best way to experience them. Next we'll look at making cordials in depth, and how to take them to the next level.

CHAPTER

9

THE
SWEET
WATER
OF LIFE

Cordials &
the Art
of Finishing

The drink that changed my life and set me on a path to making beverages for other people was the root beer float in all its sweet, delicious, flavor-dance-in-your-mouth pleasure. I was eleven years old. There was a "snack shack" at the local swimming pool, which was right down the street from my house, and I figured if I worked at the snack shack during the summer, I could learn how to make this delicious beverage and impress the girls who frequented the pool all summer. Plus, I'd get root beer floats for a quarter. When I started working there, school was still in session and my elementary school was just across the creek from the pool. Late in the spring, the shack began opening right after school got out to ply the kids with Snickers, hot dogs, and plenty of root beer floats as the pool drew closer to opening day in early May. My teacher, unaware of my plan to work my way into the hearts of all the local girls through their sweet tooths, thought of me as an enterprising, hardworking young kid and graciously let me out of school before anyone else so I could sprint over the creek and get to my post at the snack shack. Once school let out and the sound of swinging tetherballs rang through the air like wind chimes in the distance, kids would come running, a line would form, and I would get my first taste of being "in the weeds." I still remember feeling stressed about trying to carry out a hot dog order and make a root beer float at the same time.

As the pool opened and the summer wore on, I developed my own "secret" to the root beer float. To me, it was all about the temperature of the vanilla ice cream. If it was too cold, the root beer would bounce off the mounds of ice cream and create these icy little root beer crystals, which were cool on their own but also seemed to take away from the pleasure that comes from tasting the full integration of the root beer and the vanilla. Before I poured the root beer, I wanted to see a nice sheen on the ice cream as it began to melt, which allowed the root beer to slide down the ice cream and into the glass. Can't you just see the slow-motion commercial right now? If the root beer is nice and cold, which it should be, it helps to hold the ice cream at this temperature, allowing it to melt slowly and integrate itself into the beverage, taking you on a journey of flavor explosion until you're left with some crucial decisions when you get near the bottom of the glass. Do you drink it so fast that you'll need a spoon to eat the ice cream? Do you try to evenly distribute the root beer and ice cream toward the end (my preferred method) to create a satisfying final gulp of flavor bomb in your mouth? Do you patiently allow the ice cream to completely melt, leaving yourself with a shot of cream-soda-meets-root-beer at the end? Do I sound like Guy Fieri on a root beer float bender? There are so many details to think about in a simple two-ingredient drink. But it is these little secrets of flavor integration, the details that only the mildly obsessive (or, insane?) think about as they lay in bed at night, that can make the difference between a good drink and a great one. Whether it's adding a splash of ginger ale to a strawberry pie, perfecting a Mai Tai with a tiny bit of orange juice and the lightest touch of salt, or finishing al dente English peas with mint and a sprinkle of sugar, there are tiny little secrets to making anything. The more I navigate through the world of food and beverage, the more I learn and appreciate these little tricks of the trade that sprout up like dandelions. We'll explore some of these finishing touches in this chapter, focusing on the art of making cordials and liqueurs.

Chef Brian Baxter, my compadre who introduced me to the shiso-blueberry affinity in chapter 8 and also happens to be my eternal foraging buddy (it feels better walking through mysterious woods with a guy the size of a linebacker), is a master at adding complexity and depth of flavor to anything he is making. He influenced me in a big way when it came to the concept of "finishing," whether I'm making a cordial, shrub, or bitters. Chef Baxter, aside from being a visionary creatively speaking, is also very skilled and thoughtful when it comes to his dishes. In a dish of beef short ribs with beets and celery, he may try and sneak in some apple flavor by straining the beet juice glaze through some diced up apples just to kick things up a notch. Many chefs employ these little strokes of wisdom when getting a dish from conception and inspiration to execution and plating. You can do the same thing with your cordials and elixirs—starting with a root beer cordial that will become more involved as we get to the finishing stage.

VINEGAR: THE ACID TEST

Another tool that can have an amazing effect on cordials and is also the key ingredient to shrubs (drinking vinegars, which we'll get into on page 180) is acid. Acetic acid can add a lightning strike of flavor to anything, from a hint of rice wine vinegar in a plum sauce for duck to that crucial zing of lemon juice in hollandaise sauce. Adding acid to your cordials, whether through a squeeze of lemon juice or a few dashes of a concentrated vinegar, can also help you cut down on how much citrus juice you'll need to use in your cocktails. For example, if you have an idea for a whiskey and basil smash cocktail, but you're finding that the lemon juice in the drink is overpowering the basil and the whiskey, you can make a basil cordial with a hint of white vinegar, which will give the resulting drink more acid and allow you to cut back the amount of lemon juice in the cocktail by half.

I mentioned the merits of Chef Baxter earlier, and it was his partner in crime and eventual successor as Chef de Cuisine at Husk, Nate Leonard, who expanded the pantry at Husk by making so many vibrantly delicious vinegars that we suddenly had a plethora of options to finish our cordials and add to our shrubs, much to his chagrin (what can I say, he was protective of his precious elixirs). Making a melon cordial? Finish it with some lime zest and a cantaloupe vinegar. Cooking down fresh pine for a syrup with rosemary and thyme? Add some Virginia pine vinegar for a complex layer of flavor. Once Chef Nate took off on his vinegar quest, we had a closet full of bubbling, lively flavors, and the possibilities became endless. I sat down with Nate, who is in the process of starting Open Air Provisions, (you guessed it) a vinegar and provisions company, to talk about vinegars and the relatively simple process of making your own.

ME: How did you get started making vinegars? Was it just a necessity to expand the pantry and give you more options as a chef?

NATE: Yeah, it got to the point where we were buying a lot of really tasty but extremely expensive vinegars, all while dreaming up our own crazy flavors and thinking "wouldn't it be cool to have different flavor combinations that aren't available?" Then Chef Brock challenged me to just make them in house and I took off from there.

ME: With the popularity of shows and books like *Salt, Fat, Acid, Heat*, it seems like professionals and home cooks alike are realizing how important acid can be to balancing dishes and beverages. How crucial was it to your creation of dishes while you were at Husk?

NATE: It was huge. Most commercial vinegars are between 4 and 5 percent acidity. We experimented a lot with using vinegars with up to 25 percent acidity and it gives everything, especially vegetables, a lot of pop when you first taste something. When I began to make all these different vinegars, it gave me a lot of options to add new layers to different dishes.

ME: What are some tools that bartenders, chefs, and home enthusiasts can use to begin the adventure of making vinegars?

ROOT BEER CORDIAL

1 quart water

1 quart organic sugar

2 cups dried sarsaparilla root
(available online and at most home brew stores)

2 cups sassafras root

1 star anise pod

1 vanilla pod,
split open with a knife
and seeds scraped out

2 dashes of Angostura bitters
(for a little cinnamon kick and to deepen the color)

Large pinch of Maldon sea salt

Freshly ground black pepper

In a large pot, bring the water to a slow boil, then turn the heat down to a medium simmer for a few minutes. Add the sugar, stirring to incorporate, then the sarsaparilla root, sassafras root, star anise, vanilla pod and seeds, Angostura, and salt.

Allow the cordial to simmer for 20 minutes, then remove from the heat. Grind a few turns of black pepper into the mixture, and transfer to the refrigerator to steep for 2 days. If you taste the cordial after a few days and want a deeper flavor, allow it to sit for another day or two. When the cordial is ready, finish as desired (see below), then strain, bottle, and store in the refrigerator for up to 2 months, 1 month if omitting alcohol.

Here's where we get to some fun and interesting ways to add layers of additional flavor in the "finishing" stage and take the cordial into new realms. Finishing all comes down to trusting your gut and your palate to determine what can take something from good to incredible. For the root beer cordial, if you taste it after it has steeped for a few days and you're over-the-moon happy about it, just strain it and start drizzling it over ice cream or using it in whiskey sours. But if the flavor is too spiced or too "dark" for your liking, try throwing in some orange or lemon zest to give it a light citrus note and to brighten up the flavor of the cordial. Think about flavor affinity when you add these tiny layers of flavor, to avoid sacrificing the main flavor you're after in the first place. Another thing to think about when adding finishing touches is, what kind of drinks or recipes are you going to be using this cordial with? That can point you in some new directions. Here are some finishing ideas that can be applied to this root beer cordial and to different cordials as well:

For a spicier root beer flavor, first strain the original mixture, then add some broken-up cinnamon sticks (smashed with the back of a skillet), a few more star anise pods (maybe you're going to make a tiki drink with a little absinthe with this cordial?), and a few cloves. Let it sit for a few hours, then strain out the spices.

If you'd like more vanilla flavor, add ½ teaspoon vanilla extract and another vanilla pod, let sit for 6 hours, then strain the mixture.

For a more herbaceous root beer cordial (mint and wintergreen are common in root beer recipes), add some fresh mint and rosemary, let the mixture sit for another 4 to 6 hours, and strain.

Finally, if you taste your cordial and want a more classic soda shop flavor, in a saucepan, slowly cook down 6 ounces of your favorite root beer soda until you're left with only an ounce, let that cool, and strain it into your root beer cordial.

NATE: You will definitely need a pH meter, which you can buy online for around 40 bucks. You can make small-batch vinegars in half-gallon mason jars. You'll need some cheesecloth and some Braggs unfiltered apple cider vinegar, for the mother. Once you've made some vinegars you can use the mother from those.

ME: Can you take us through some techniques for making your own vinegar at home?

NATE: Well, there are essentially three basic methods for making your own vinegar, so I'll start with a very simple method, which is infusion. Go and buy some distilled white vinegar and infuse whichever ingredient you want into it for anywhere from 7 days to 3 to 4 weeks. Soft herbs like mint, basil, and lemon balm won't take too long to assert their flavor, while firmer ingredients like apples or vegetables may take up to a month. Strain and bottle and you have your own flavored vinegar.

Another method is the two-step process, in which you basically make your own country wine using a product that already has residual sugar, like blackberries, watermelon, cantaloupe, or grapes. This is where the hydrometer comes into play. You juice or mash the fruit, then take a reading of that product, which will determine the alcohol potential of the vinegar-to-be. Write down that number because you will take another reading after fermentation. To begin the fermentation process, add the fruit mash to your half-gallon mason jar, add some champagne yeast, and allow that sugar to convert to alcohol, which will take a few days. Take a reading with the hydrometer after a few days. If you got a reading of 15 before fermentation and a reading of 1 after fermentation, your alcohol level is 14 (15 minus 1). 15 percent is the goal. Then weigh the mixture with a digital scale and add 10 percent of the weight in sugar, and 4 percent in mother (Braggs unfiltered or mother from a different vinegar). Allow that to sit for about a month in a cool, dark place away from sunlight, then strain into another clean half-gallon Mason jar, cap, and label.

The last method is the one-step process, which I use a lot and would be quite helpful for people who want to use herbs and other things from the garden to make vinegars. The goal again is 15 percent alcohol, 10 percent sugar, and 4 percent mother. Here's an example of how to use the one-step process to make Chamomile Vinegar, but you can substitute any fresh herbs or flowers that you may have growing.

One of the most common ways to use vinegar in beverages is by making shrubs. In culinary parlance, the word shrub basically means "drinking vinegar." Shrubs were very popular in colonial times, both to slake an overworked thirst and to help preserve fruit in beverage form. Most shrubs are made up of three simple ingredients: sugar, vinegar, and any fruit or vegetable. In my experience, they are best employed in the summer months, when berries are plentiful and in season, and when drinks with that extra-acidic tang help serve the purpose of cooling you down. There are two methods for making shrubs: the hot process, in which ingredients are cooked, and the cold process, in which ingredients are steeped for a time and stirred. Since we'll be using in-season fruit and delicate herbs, I would highly recommend sticking with the cold process method to make your shrubs more vibrant. Cold processing also allows the oils and aromatics of any ingredients you use to remain intact throughout the infusion process, instead of running the risk of cooking out that flavor. One basic ratio for shrubs is to use equal parts fruit or vegetable, sugar, and vinegar in a drawn-out infusion process over a few weeks. However, if you're using stronger vinegars like balsamic or apple cider vinegar instead of just white distilled, you may want to use less vinegar; in the equal-parts ratio

CHAMOMILE VINEGAR

4 cups of dry, unoaked white wine

½ cup sugar

2½ tablespoons mother
(Braggs unfiltered cider vinegar)

3 tablespoons fresh chamomile

1½ tablespoons dried chamomile

Combine all ingredients in a half-gallon Mason jar. Stretch a piece of cheesecloth over the top, and attach the outer ring of the lid to keep the cheesecloth in place, but also allow for open-air circulation. Keep the jar away from sunlight in a cool, dark place where the temperature won't exceed 74 degrees F. Check the acidity after 30 days. The vinegar can be left to do its magic for 60 to 90 days, by which point the mother will have has done most of its work. After that, leaving the vinegar for longer will only lead you to lose some water to evaporation, increasing the concentration, flavor, and acidity. Once you've reached maturity with the vinegar and are happy with the taste and concentration, strain the mixture by doing a "gravity strain," which is a simple method where you don't press any solids or force any more extraction. This will keep the vinegar from being too cloudy. Store in a mason jar with the lid on, labeled and dated, for up to 6 months.

This homemade chamomile vinegar is perfect for use in all kinds of beverages. Adding a splash to some herbal tea would be akin to squeezing a bit of lemon into it, but it would add a delicious jolt of herbal acidity. It could also provide a valuable finishing touch to many different cordials, syrups, and cocktails. Here are a few examples:

- Add 2 tablespoons of the chamomile vinegar to a quart of fresh chamomile-infused honey syrup (2 parts honey to 1 part water).

- Add I tablespoon of chamomile vinegar to a pint of any herbaceous syrup, like lemon verbena or mint syrup. It will add a soft floral note and serve to round out the flavor.

- Put the chamomile vinegar in a dasher bottle and use similar to bitters. Adding a few dashes to an egg white cocktail adds a beautiful layer of complexity. Even in an old fashioned (pictured), that light chamomile flavor adds a summery twist, especially combined with sorghum.

a stronger vinegar can overtake the aroma of any cocktail you make with it. Here's a cold-process recipe for Strawberry-Basil Shrub (page 187), which can be adapted to different fruit-herb combinations like Blueberry-Lemon Verbena or Blackberry-Lavender.

FRESH VERSUS DRIED HERBS (AND USING THEM BOTH)

When deciding between fresh and dried herbs in your cordials, assuming you have both available, fresh is usually your best bet for use in cold cocktails. Dried herbs are great for teas and hot drinks and can be ground into powders to use for rims and other garnishing ideas. But using a small amount of dried herbs in conjunction with fresh can provide more structure and depth to the finished product. Take this Lavender Orange Blossom Cordial, which uses orange blossom honey to accentuate the floral qualities of the lavender and the flavor affinity it shares with honey in general. We can add depth to it by adding some dried lavender, while "finishing" the cordial by straining it through more fresh lavender and adding some orange zest to bolster the orange flavor in the honey.

STRAWBERRY-BASIL SHRUB

I quart halved strawberries,
including the tops

I quart organic sugar

I quart distilled white vinegar

I ounce lemon juice

I cup loosely packed basil leaves
(some basil flowers thrown in would be lovely!)

3 flowering dandelions

2 sprigs of parsley

I tablespoon basil seeds

Place the halved strawberries in a sterilized container and add the sugar on top. Let the mixture sit in the fridge for a few days, then add the rest of the ingredients and whisk to combine. Return the mixture to the refrigerator and let it infuse for a week, checking it for strength after 3 to 4 days. When you're happy with the flavor, strain, bottle, and store in the refrigerator for up to 2 months.

STRAWBERRY-BASIL COOLER WITH GINGER

2 ounces of a good spicy ginger soda
like Blenheim

2 ounces Strawberry-Basil Shrub (page 187)

1 strawberry, quartered,
tops left on

2 basil leaves, divided

Soda water
(preferably Topo Chico), to top

Dandelion flowers

Fill a tall glass with plenty of ice. Add the ginger soda
and shrub, strawberry, and one of the basil leaves, stir,
and top with the soda water. Garnish with a basil leaf
and dandelions and serve with a straw.

LAVENDER-ORANGE BLOSSOM CORDIAL

1 quart orange blossom honey

1 pint water

¼ cup dried lavender

2 drops orange flower water

8 sprigs of lavender, flowers and all,
plus more for finishing

Zest of 1 orange

Combine the honey and water over low heat to incorporate the two, then add the dried lavender as it cools. After the syrup has cooled and the dried lavender has infused for 30 minutes, add the orange flower water and fresh lavender and stir to combine. Transfer to the refrigerator to infuse. The next day, add a few more sprigs of lavender and the orange zest. Leave the finishing ingredients in for 15 minutes, then strain the mixture and bottle it. The cordial will keep for 2 months in the refrigerator.

GARDEN TO GLASS "CHARTREUSE"

1 cup Virginia pine needles

1 cup wildflowers
(clover, violet, honeysuckle, wisteria)

1 large handful of fresh mint leaves

1 large handful of fresh lemon verbena leaves

1 large handful of fresh lemon balm leaves

½ cup fresh dill, leaves and flowers

½ cup fresh chamomile flowers

2 sprigs of rosemary

2 sprigs of lavender

2 sprigs of thyme

3 tablespoons grated lemon zest
(use a microplane)

4 tablespoons fresh dandelion flower

2 tablespoons fresh basil,
leaves and flowers

1 tablespoon fresh tansy

¼ cup dried chamomile

1 tablespoon dried mint

1 tablespoon dried Angelica root

1 teaspoon dried dandelion root

1 teaspoon pink peppercorns

1 teaspoon basil seed

1 teaspoon saffron

1 teaspoon dried dill

2 cardamom pods, cracked

2 star anise pods

120 ounces 100 proof vodka

½ cup local honey

Combine all the ingredients except the vodka and honey in a large gallon mason jar. Add the vodka and cover with the lid. Shake the mixture a few times and let sit in a cool, dark area for 2 weeks. Come back to the mixture when you can and shake it to agitate the ingredients for a better extraction. After 2 weeks, strain the mixture through cheesecloth, squeezing the cloth to extract as much flavor as possible. If you're satisfied with the flavor of the extraction, add the honey, bottle, and begin dreaming up new cocktails to make. The elixir will keep at room temperature for months. To take your Chartreuse to another level, simply add more fresh and dried ingredients and infuse for 2 more weeks. I like to add another layer of lemon flavor by doing a second infusion with more lemon verbena, lemon balm, and lemon zest. This can be a great way to brighten up the deep, complex flavors from the first infusion. Or, if you'd like a more minty flavor, add some fresh mint (maybe some chocolate mint?) for a second infusion. Interested in a floral Chartreuse? Try adding rose petals, violets, marigolds, and any flowering herb you may have in the garden. If you'd like a sweeter flavor profile, try adding some rich simple syrup (2 parts sugar to 1 part water) to keep the honey flavor from taking over. Some prefer the honeyed, more mellow taste of yellow Chartreuse while some love the bold, peppery intensity of green. Experiment with different batches and keep notes of which ingredients "pop." This can also nudge you in a certain direction for that perfect cocktail to make with your Chartreuse.

GARDEN TO GLASS
DILL SOUR

1¼ ounces Linie Acquavit

½ ounce blanco tequila

½ ounce Garden to Glass "Chartreuse" (page 190)
(or equal parts yellow and green Chartreuse)

½ ounce lemon juice

¼ ounce lime juice

½ ounce Dill Flower Cordial (page 196)

½ ounce heavy cream

1 egg white

Tiny pinch of Maldon sea salt

1 dill straw (see Note)
and some dill flowers, for garnish

Combine all ingredients in a shaker without ice and shake vigorously to incorporate the egg white and the cream. Add a few large pieces of ice to the tin and shake again for around 30 seconds, or until the tin is so cold you can barely hold on to it. Strain the cocktail into a Collins glass or Mason jar and serve neat (without ice). Similar to the Ramos Gin Fizz, this is like drinking a cloud. Since the drink will have a nice white "head" on it from the egg white and cream, you can easily tuck some beautifully aromatic dill flowers around the top of the drink for garnish, and serve with the dill straw.

NOTE: To create dill "straws," cut a large stalk of dill from your garden and trim the flower heads and leaves to reserve for garnish. Notice the occasional notches in the long stalk. Use these as your guide to cut 5- to 6-inch pieces to use as dill drinking straws. Once cut, keep the dill straws in a plastic bag in the refrigerator, or in a cup of water if you're planning on using them all within a few days.

HEY, HEY, WE'RE THE MONKS

Though their secrets will probably never be known, the monks of the Grand Chartreuse Mountains know plenty about the art of cordials and liqueurs. Outside the city of Voiron, France, nestled in the tall, jagged mountains that give the monastery its name, the monks live in solitude, praying in silence for up to eight hours a day and spending a lot of time alone. This is a place, to quote Kris Kristofferson, where "lonesome is more than a state of mind." The fact that they produce one of the oldest, most revered, and most complicated alchemical elixirs known to man is both fascinating and improbable. I like to imagine a group of robed Jedi warriors of the herbal arts, roaming the countryside while carrying large baskets of freshly picked wildflowers and curious herbs, all for the purpose of making an elixir initially thought to prolong one's life. The recipe for Green Chartreuse, which reportedly consists of more than 130 different ingredients, macerated in up to seven separate combinations before being blended, distilled, and aged, is one of the holy grails of alchemy. The recipe has been passed down over generations and is known by only two of the monks at the Grand Chartreuse Monastery at any given time. The monks who acquire the recipe take an oath of secrecy, and unlike that new Frank Ocean single, it has never leaked out beyond the grand stone walls of the distillery. The easiest answer to the question, "What is in Chartreuse?" is: everything.

While we may never know the recipe, one thing we can learn from the monks of the Grand Chartreuse is how to foster a collaborative growing and foraging program in order to diversify the amount of ingredients available to us at any given time. There are different herb gardens around the monastery site in Voiron, to keep the distillery plied with the ingredients it needs to produce its vaunted liqueurs. Restaurant and bar managers and cocktail program creators can draw inspiration from this approach to better source the botanicals they need to keep their offerings fresh and dynamic. When I was bar manager at Husk, and while preparing to open Chopper, my new tiki project in East Nashville, each year I would try to divvy up who was growing what on the staff in order to have more ingredients at our disposal that we wouldn't have to order from restaurant supply companies. This ensures that no matter what ingredients you're using, the end product is going to taste better, have more flavor, and last longer. And the ability to use specific parts of a plant at different stages of its growth can inspire all kinds of creativity.

We had a lot of success growing dill mostly for the flowers, since they infuse beautifully into cordials and syrups, giving a pleasant cooling, creamy sensation that we couldn't get from any other plant. Eventually we noticed the stalks getting so big we could use them for straws, due to their hollowed-out structure. This was an instance where we went against traditional gardening wisdom (cutting back an herb when it gets close to going to seed) in order to make a beverage we wouldn't have expected to create when we started growing dill. And by going through this journey as the plant grew, we were able to pick up all kinds of different flavors, from the stem to the flower to the seed, which helped me make a cocktail that touched on these different flavors and helped accentuate them (see page 190). It's amazing to watch and taste how a plant changes as it passes through its growing cycle.

But if you want to feel like a monk who's at peace with his surroundings, try to make your own "chartreuse" using your garden, pantry, and whatever else you can find growing in your environment. This homemade Chartreuse recipe (see page 190) can be adapted to whatever is growing in your garden or thriving in your area. You'll notice it's pretty difficult to even source 130 ingredients, so the kitchen-sink method can serve you well here. Have some cloves sitting in your pantry that you only use at Christmastime? Use them.

DILL FLOWER
CORDIAL

3 cups sugar

1½ cups water

¼ teaspoon kosher salt

2 teaspoons white distilled vinegar

2 cups dill flowers

½ cup dill leaves, chopped

3 tablespoons grated lemon zest
(use a Microplane)

Combine the sugar, water, and salt in a saucepan and bring to a mild simmer, stirring to incorporate the sugar. Once incorporated, remove the pan from the heat and add the vinegar. Let the syrup completely cool in the refrigerator, so as not to sully the fresh, vibrant flavor and aroma of the dill. When cool, add the dill flowers and leaves. Then add the lemon zest and let the cordial infuse, in the refrigerator for 2 to 3 days, until the taste is vibrant and floral. Strain, bottle, and keep in the refrigerator for 2 months.

Is there chickweed, a wild herb that tastes like fresh English peas, growing all over your yard? Yep, use it. Just remember, don't use anything that has been sprayed with pesticides. And if you can't identify it, don't use it. If you'd like to use more fresh ingredients than dry, replace the dry ingredients in the recipe with three times as much fresh. I want to give props to Colby Rasavong, an amazing chef based in Brooklyn, who pushed me to make a batch based on an old recipe that had been passed down to him. His old recipe had about eight ingredients, which I just didn't think was quite Chartreusian enough. (Take note, this should not be consumed by anyone pregnant or wanting to get pregnant. The herb tansy, has been shown to decrease fertility in women, and was used by Native Americans for this [among other] purposes.)

If I've given you too many ingredients to find and grow at this point, and you're thinking, "Who does this guy think I am, some herbalist Gandalf with a robe, magic wand and satchel full of herbs?" despair not. Nobody can grow it all, sometimes it helps to know some wise farmers (see page 63 for the Barefoot Farmer's wisdom) who, just like us, are always learning and have plenty of gardening advice and delicious produce.

CHAPTER

10

KNOW YOUR ROOTS & YOUR FARMERS

When I began to explore the beautiful symbiotic relationship between ginger and cayenne in more depth, I started asking around town, talking to chefs, farmers, and purveyors about sourcing these ingredients in the freshest way possible. This led me to Earth Advocates Research Farm, located just south of Franklin, Tennessee, who sold their extremely unique produce at the Franklin Farmer's Market every Saturday. I had heard they were growing ginger and harvesting in the fall, selling it with the long stalks and leaves, which have their own pleasant, floral, lemongrassy aroma, still attached. When I visited their tent one Saturday in late September, it was like entering a world I didn't know existed in Middle Tennessee. There was the strange Japanese fruit, akebia quintata, with a small tan husk like a coin purse, opening up to a strange fruit which resembled a caterpillar. I smelled some "dragon citrus," an extremely bitter variety most sought-after for the peels, which smelled like a bed of roses with a hint of lemon and grapefruit. Other plants that stood out were the blue balsam mint, with a cooling wintergreen aroma, and some locally grown passionfruit. But what most people had come for was the pile of fragrant young ginger and turmeric they had grown, so fresh since it had been harvested a day earlier. There was a discernible difference between this ginger and the ginger you'll find at the grocery store. And the benefit of having the leaves intact for making teas or using for garnish, as I did in a Corn n' Oil riff (rum, lime, and falernum) with muddled fresh ginger, made this drink special and more experiential.

Now, I'm not saying that everyone needs to go out and find somebody who is growing ginger, turmeric, and other exotic ingredients. But if there is an ingredient that interests you as you begin to go down the rabbit hole trying to find the best source possible, you will most likely need to get closer to the actual grower or producer of that product. And what you'll often find are many other ingredients you either didn't know existed or had no idea grew close by. In my search for wild ginger, or just fresher ginger in general, I had a whole world of ingredients open up to me through Earth Advocates, and now I've been growing their blue balsam mint for a few years and there is simply nothing like it. I used the dragon citrus for bitters and infused the peels into some floral pisco, and I made a very strange, peppery passionfruit cordial, which wouldn't have been possible without immersing myself into the freshness of that ingredient.

You may have heard the saying, "No Farms, No Food," and in my case this has been quite literally true—there have been numerous times where a purveyor or a large producer couldn't get something I was after, so I had to go straight to the farms myself. And that process has turned me on to dynamic new ingredients. At that same Franklin Farmers Market, one of the best places to buy produce and meat in the Middle Tennessee region, I would turn around and see the amazing and kind folks of Bear Creek Farm, producing what many chefs believe to be the finest beef in America. Then I'd walk by the Bloomsbury Farms stand to pick up persimmons, which tasted like pumpkin pie and whiskey, and visit the Mennonite family who picked beautiful watercress at the river's edge and sold milk perfect for making cheese. Even something as simple as the search for a fine strawberry can open up new worlds of flavor and discovery. I took my family to Delvin Farms in Nashville to pick our own strawberries, and we left with a bunch of nasturtium starter plants, which later became my daughter's favorite herb (and a way to get her to eat "salad"!) and made for a striking cocktail garnish when it flowered.

Some of the most special people I've met are farmers and growers, and there are even a few who have become great friends, like Chris, Tracy, and Winston from White Squirrel Farm, located north of Nashville in Bethpage, Tennessee. Prominently featured on the menu at restaurants like Lockeland Table and Graze in Nashville,

White Squirrel Farm also produce skin care products and a delicious carrot-habanero hot sauce, all made by hand with ingredients grown on their farm. I first met them at a local market where they were selling baby heirloom squash that was so delicious I had a *moment* when I ate it. I stopped cold in the kitchen, thinking, "What's going on here?" So I kept going back week after week and eventually realized that Winston, the farmers' Kung Fu-kickin', artistic talent-bursting son was a fan of both Neil Young and Bunny Wailer, as was I. Chris would tell stories of living in Jamaica and having other adventures around the world, learning from shamans. I would query him about the strange brews he'd had from Bangkok to Bowling Green, and he would give me little gardening tips along the way. We would buy Tracy's homemade skin care items and deodorants, and if I got out of line, little Winston might give me a swift kick in the... shins. I sat down with the folks from White Squirrel Farm to talk farming, gardening, and learning to let nature take control.

MW: Your neighbor to the North, Jeff Poppin, the Barefoot Farmer (page 63) talks about how farming and being a musician are similar in that they both appeal to folks who want to bypass the 9 to 5 office job. What inspired you to become farmers?

CHRIS, of White Squirrel Farm: Oh man, it's more like a 5 am to 9 pm! I'd love to only work 9 to 5, to be honest! But you don't do this to *not* work, that's for sure. Farming was our way to be home with our son and spend time together as a family. I came up with the idea that I would be a farmer when I was young but I didn't realize how hard it was. It was a fleeting thought.

TRACY, of White Squirrel Farm: We're 7 years in and we still feel like beginners. We make the rules, and we constantly learn about what works best in what season. It's nice to not really have a boss.

CHRIS: Nature is our boss here (laughs). You're at the mercy of all those crazy cycles. Nature can be an emotional roller-coaster, but it makes you appreciate the different seasons and growing cycles.

TRACY: It makes you appreciate how intense it can be to get a plant from the seed to eventually taking it to market.

MW: What advice can you lend to the home gardener or novice looking to grow their own food?

TRACY: Experience is the teacher; if you're not doing it, how can you learn about it? I would say that growing things eventually teaches you to not grow too attached to what you're growing. There are so many things that are out of your control and you begin to feel like it's all teaching you a big lesson.

CHRIS: Overall, plants are always teaching us. You get better at accepting failure, that's for sure. It's been good for me to try to let go of some things that I can't control. There are all of these Daoist lessons in growing things.

MW: Do you have a favorite plant that you grow, a vegetable or an herb that speaks to you year in and year out?

TRACY: If I had to pick a favorite these days, I'd have to say Yarrow. I love it because it's a perennial and you can plant it once and it will come back year after year. The flowers are beautiful and it's medicinal; you can use it for skin care products, teas and drinks. There are so many different colors as well. When we first moved to Bethpage and started our farm, we noticed how yarrow grew wild all over our property. Butterflies really take to it as well.

GINGER-CAYENNE CORDIAL

2 cups water

1 cup dry white wine

3 cups white sugar

2 cups julienned ginger (peeled and diced)

2 tablespoons ginger juice

1 tablespoon lemon juice

1 dried cayenne pepper,
(handled with gloves!) split open and
coarsely chopped on a separate cutting board

Start with the water, adding it to a pot and simmering over medium-high heat. Add the wine and cook for 5 minutes until the smell of alcohol dissipates. Turn the heat down to a light simmer and add the sugar, and ginger, stirring to incorporate. Remove from heat after a few minutes and allow to cool, then add the ginger juice, lemon juice, and dried cayenne pepper. Let that mixture steep for 3 days or until the heat/spice level of the cordial is to your liking. The purpose of the cayenne is to mimic and intensify the spicy character of raw ginger. Using dried cayenne adds an element of umami that gives a lot of depth to this cordial.

MW: Yarrow is a great example of a plant that grows wild all across North America (with tiny white flowers), but can also be easily grown in the garden with gorgeous pink and purple varieties. You grow a lot of flowers at White Squirrel. Is that so you've got a mix of flowers and vegetables to bring to market?

TRACY: Growing herbs and flowers along with your vegetables helps draw pollinators to your garden. We don't sell that many flowers but we do grow a lot. I try to position them near plants like squash and cucumber to draw the pollinators closer to those plants.

MW: One of my favorite things to get at your market stand are the dried cayenne peppers. They give such a big flavor boost to anything I use them in. What do you use the dried peppers for?

TRACY: We make a carrot hot sauce with peppers that is pretty popular. But I think you're the only one who uses the dried cayenne (laughs).

Every bartender should have a cocktail in their arsenal that plays to service industry pros and serious cocktail drinkers. Something for those who put the *spirit* in spirituous, a dynamic drink to jolt the mind and body. Using peppers, whether fresh or dried, affords the bartender the opportunity to add heat and excitement to any cocktail. These drinks are the kinds of drinks bartenders make for other bartenders. You think you want a margarita on your day off? Try enlivening that sullied, tired palate with this drink, the Day-Off Rita, inspired by those gas station cans of beer-rita, which purport to have big flavors of cranberry, pineapple, and coconut, but actually just taste like carbonated cough medicine.

DAY-OFF RITA
(ONE FOR THE BARTENDERS)

1½ ounces Reposado Tequila

1 ounce Mezcal

⅜ ounce fresh lime juice

⅜ ounce fresh lemon juice

½ ounce ginger cayenne cordial

Barspoon (⅛ ounce) Green Chartreuse

Barspoon (⅛ ounce) Giffard Pineapple Liqueur

Small pinch of salt

1 ounce Topo Chico sparkling water

Ginger leaves, pineapple fronds,
and mint (optional), for garnish

Shake all ingredients with plenty of ice and open
pour into a tall glass. Garnish with ginger leaves,
pineapple fronds, or mint. Sip slowly.

WORKING WITH YARROW,
THE FARMER'S FRIEND

As Tracy from White Squirrel discussed, yarrow can be a very useful plant in the garden, the kitchen, and even in the bar. While gentian root (page 32) is available to order online to use for bitters and cordials, yarrow flower buds are another fresh bittering agent to add to your arsenal. They can be sprinkled on top of a sweet drink served in a coupe glass, to add a counterpoint to the overall taste of the cocktail. The drink can be sweet, then when one takes a sip with a small yarrow flower bud in it, the pleasant floral bitterness completely changes the sensation in your mouth. Yarrow flowers can serve two functions in a bitters recipe: to add floral character as well as long-lasting bitterness. It's also a plant that will last deep into summertime and fall, when the season changes as the cold nights settle in and you're left with leaves drifting from the trees and flowers falling over or going to seed.

CHAPTER

11

AS
the
SEASONS
ROLL

I nevitably there comes a time, if you live in an area of the world with seasons, where you venture out to the garden to fetch some herbs for dinner, a few flowers for the table, or a late-season pepper or two, and the garden just looks *sad*. Overcooked and falling over sideways like a drunk dancer at a wedding, as deep brown colors of the earth begin to show up on the stalks of herbs and vegetables and the promise of May and June gives way to the slow death of October and November. Luckily, depending on which growing zone you live in, there are plenty of hardy herbs and vegetables that can help you get through the winter and keep your drinking game dynamic and fresh. Clear your head by clearing some space where the flowering cucumbers were growing months earlier, turning the soil over, and amending it with some compost and manure-bolstered soil. Then, as long as the area gets around four hours of sun in the colder months, you can begin to expand your winter palate by planting herbs such as winter savory, rosemary, thyme, different sages like watermelon sage, and even parsley. Before that planet of rhubarb begins to unfurl from the soil in March, there are still joys to be had in the winter garden—as well as plenty of methods for preserving the past season's bounty.

If you live in a northern part of the country, say, Minneapolis, which I love, and there aren't many options for fresh ingredients throughout the winter, you can look into hydroponic growing operations and microgreen producers, who can provide a wealth of fresh, unique ingredients even in the dead of winter. In Nashville, we're lucky to have a guy like Tom Maddox of Carter Creek Greens, who's not only one of the most fun guys to sit and have a beer with, he's also passionate about growing things and providing exciting and inspiring ingredients to chefs and bartenders around the city. No matter how obscure the plant, if you've heard about it and you want Tom to give it a shot, he'll do days of research to figure out if he can grow it. I sat down with Tom, who grows microgreens in an indoor facility downtown as well as other plants on a farm 20 minutes outside of town, providing local chefs and bartenders with a variety of herbs no matter the season.

MW: How did you get your start growing things?

TOM: I've always been a farmer; I grew up as a farmer. My mom and dad always grew things at the house, and there was always talk of how the seasons blend into different plants, how planting things at certain times was important, and above all, how you had to take care of the soil. From the time I was eight years old up until now, the garden has always been an adventure for us as a family, and a constant presence in my home. My grandparents were planting tobacco, corn, soy, and it always stuck with me. I love planting things. I want to plant things that make people happy.

MW: What advice might you have for a gardener wanting to make their soil better?

TOM: If you make coffee at your house, keep all your coffee grounds. If you use eggs, keep all of your egg shells. When everything builds up, it makes for a great compost. Those two things are common in most households and they make for a great way to start amending your soil and give your garden a boost.

MW: What's something you have grown that has informed your overall approach to gardening?

TOM: I would have to say lemon verbena. It can be such a difficult plant, but what I have been taught out of that plant is an incredible thing because of what it does, how it grows, and what it can provide in terms of flavor and aroma. African Blue Basil is another that is one of the greatest basils I've ever come across and will just keep growing late in the summer and into fall. The color of it and the leaf shape are so beautiful and there is a hint of cinnamon and anise that is unlike anything else. And by the time it's grown up and big, it's like a kid in high school who's all confident and tells you, "What's up, man? Check me out, I'm awesome!" So many chefs love the buds of African Blue Basil so much because there is an incredible amount of flavor in them. There is a cumin–meets-cinnamon-meets-hard spice flavor that is just so much fun.

MW: What are some other favorite herbs of yours?

TOM: Every basil; for instance, lime basil is so amazing because it's a flavor you're not going to find anywhere else. It's not just lime and basil, it's a combination of so many things. Borage flowers are also an amazingly awesome thing to watch grow and give color and invite pollinators to the garden.

MW: Is there something you've grown that had a different use that you didn't expect? Like my experience growing figs and using the leaves more than the actual fruit?

TOM: Growing hibiscus was interesting because I knew the flowers and leaves were amazing, but when I chewed on the stalk I realized it tasted like granny smith apple. I started showing that to different chefs and they were blown away because now they had a different flavor to use in that same plant. I love finding out new things about plants I've grown for a while.

MW: What's the most unusual plant you've tried to grow?

TOM: Six years ago, Josh Habiger (of Catbird Seat and now Chef/Owner of Bastion) came to me and said "Do you know what oyster leaf is? I'd love to use it, it's one of the coolest things you'll ever grow. If you can grow it, I'd love to use it." So a few years passed, I did cursory research here and there, I found seeds here and there and had some luck with it, but not enough to sell any. And just recently I looked at one of the plants and it was finally doing well after nursing it for three years. And it's one of the coolest, most delicious things I've ever tasted in my entire life. It's a small plant and it's not like a restaurant could use it or anything, but it's the most unique plant and most special thing I've ever tasted. It tastes like the liquid from the most delicious oyster you've ever eaten. It's the most difficult thing I've ever grown, but here I am six years later tasting it. So I've got to find a way to grow this stuff, it's just really difficult. It's the dumbest thing I've ever done, really (laughs). I mean, think about it, man! I brought this chef two leaves off this plant after six years and we both had a big laugh! I said, "What were you expecting? One hundred leaves? It didn't work out that way, man." So that's one of the most amazing growing stories that I have. It's a happy ending but the story keeps going. I absolutely love making people happy by growing things that excite them. Putting smiles on people's faces by growing things is such a great feeling.

MW: That's amazing. So, what are some things people can do in fall and winter to make their soil healthier and their garden better?

TOM: Rye is something people can grow over the winter to give the soil nutrients and put things back into the soil. In springtime it'll rise up and say, "Dang it's too damn hot out here, I'm outta here!" But what rye did was put all the nutrients back into your soil and keep it healthy for spring. And you don't have to spend much money.

FOREST TODDY

1 herbal or black tea bag,
or a small bouquet garni
of your dried homegrown herbs

1 lemon, at room temperature

½ ounce honey syrup
(2 parts honey to 1 part water)

1½ ounces good rye whiskey, or to taste
(I recommend Rittenhouse)

1 dash Angostura
or other aromatic bitters

Thyme, rosemary, and/or sage,
for garnish

In a teapot, boil enough water for two drinks. Fill up your mug with the freshly boiled water and place a plate on top to seal in the heat. After a few minutes, with the mug piping hot, discard your tempering water and fill the mug a little more than halfway with more of the freshly boiled water. Add the tea or herbs and put the plate back on top of the mug to seal in the heat and get a nice infusion going. We're going for a very mild tea/herbal flavor and don't want any astringency getting in the way of our whiskey-warming enjoyment, so let your tea infuse for 2 to 3 minutes. In the meantime, cut some small lemon wedges, discarding the seeds.

Take the plate off the top of the mug and take out the teabag or bouquet garni. Squeeze ½ ounce of fresh lemon juice into the mug, then add the honey syrup. Add the whiskey to taste and a dash of Angostura bitters. Warm a spoon under the faucet and stir well with the warm spoon. For the garnish, cut a slit in a wedge of lemon and place it on the rim of the mug, tucking your herbs into the lemon wedge to keep them neatly tucked to one side of your cup. You now have the perfect beverage to ward off seasonal affective disorder and to contemplate all the delicious things you're about to make with that fire burning in front of you.

Now that you've mastered the hot toddy and more importantly, the steps needed to get a mug hot and keep it hot, it's time to experience the silky, luxurious pleasures of the hot-buttered rum. A hot-buttered rum is the perfect vehicle for adding delicious fat (in this case, butter) to a cocktail and having it incorporate quickly and easily for your drinking enjoyment. Cold drinks don't have that luxury. In a properly executed hot-buttered rum, you're essentially fat-washing your drink without any messy straining or cloudy colors. As for the hot toddy, you'll need a mug with a handle, a small plate, and enough boiling water for double the amount of drinks you're making.

HOT SAGE-
BUTTERED RUM

½ cup water

5 dashes Angostura
or other aromatic bitters, divided

8 to 10 sage leaves,
plus some sage "trees" for garnish

6 tablespoons Kerrygold salted butter,
or any good European-style butter, softened

1 black tea bag
or a homemade bouquet garni of dried herbs

1 lemon, at room temperature

1 tablespoon honey syrup
(2 parts honey to 1 part water)

1 teaspoon St. Elizabeth's Allspice Dram
or other allspice liqueur

1 to 2 ounces good Jamaican rum
(like Appleton Estate 12 year)

Star anise pods, for garnish

AT LEAST 4 HOURS AHEAD:

In a medium saucepan, combine the water with 4 dashes of
the bitters and bring to a boil, then reduce the heat to a low
simmer. Add the sage leaves and cook for 5 to 10 minutes,
until it's nice and fragrant, being careful not to let all the
liquid evaporate. Remove from the heat and let your sage
"tea" cool down for 15 minutes. Strain out the cooked sage
leaves through a tea strainer or cheesecloth and discard.

Combine the sage tea and butter in a mixing bowl and mix, by hand using a wooden spoon or in a stand mixer fitted with the paddle attachment, until incorporated. Set out a sheet of plastic wrap on your counter and use a spatula to carefully transfer the butter mix onto the wrap. After you've gotten every bit of that delicious, aromatic butter out of the mixing bowl, roll and shape it into the shape of a stick of butter. Place it in the refrigerator for at least 4 hours or overnight to firm back up a little, to make it easy to slice into your hot-buttered rum.

WHEN READY TO DRINK:

In a teapot, boil enough water for two drinks. While your water is boiling, get the sage butter out of the refrigerator and let it sit at room temperature to soften a bit. Fill up your mug with the freshly boiled water and place a plate on top to seal in the heat. After a few minutes, discard the tempering water and fill the mug a little more than halfway with more of the freshly boiled water. Add the tea bag or herbs, and put the plate back on top of the mug to seal in the heat and get a nice infusion going. While the tea is infusing, cut some wedges of lemon, removing the seeds. After 3 minutes, remove the tea bag and lift the plate off your mug and squeeze in about ½ ounce of lemon juice. Add the honey syrup, allspice liqueur, the remaining dash of bitters, and the rum to taste, depending on how strong you like your drink. Warm a spoon under the faucet and stir all the ingredients together in the mug. Slice 2 small pats of sage butter and add them to your drink, slowly stirring to incorporate the butter (I know you're thirsty, but don't spill your precious creation by stirring too aggressively!). Garnish with a big sprig of sage, and star anise pods and use the sprig to stir in the butter as needed. Be warm, be merry—you are enjoying a drink so delicious, it doesn't matter how cold it is outside.

WARMING UP TO HOT DRINKS

As October sets in and the leaves just begin to change, aided by those first sheets of cold air drifting in from the North, the craving begins for more robust, warming beverages. And we don't have to leave our beloved herbs behind, either. This is the perfect time of year to lean on the strong aromatic herbs like rosemary, sage, and thyme to enhance savory, delicious cocktails, especially hot ones. As a bartender, I know it's time to start shifting my mind-set the first time someone scrunches their nose a little and asks "Do y'all make a hot toddy?" It's such an innocent, pure request ("I require whiskey, hot"), it's a wonder they've ever been denied such a simple pleasure. Though these are the type of seemingly easy beverages that can be difficult to pull off in any sort of volume, whether at a bar or at your first bonfire of the year, when executed correctly, they are deceptively simple little masterpieces, companions as you contemplate the changing seasons. So before we get to the pleasures of harnessing smoke and fire to enhance our drinking experience, let's master the hot toddy and hot buttered rum.

Often the most difficult and overlooked aspect of making and drinking hot cocktails is the temperature of the liquid and the mug itself. If you make a perfect hot toddy in a cold mug that hasn't been tempered (filled with boiling or very hot water to get it piping hot), the drink won't stay hot past the first few sips, defeating the purpose of drinking a hot drink in the first place. So, if you're making one hot toddy, you'll need enough hot water for two, since you'll be discarding the water you're using to temper your mug. For each hot toddy, you'll need a mug with a handle and a small plate to cover the mug. Here, we're making just one—as rocker George Thorogood once yelled, "When I drink alone, I prefer to be by myself!"

GUM SYRUP

6 ounces water, divided
2 ounces of acacia powder
(Frontier brand is widely available)
12 ounces sugar

In a small, sealable container, combine 2 ounces of the water and the acacia powder, seal, and shake lightly to incorporate. Place your container in the refrigerator and wait a day or two for the acacia powder to dissolve. Once the acacia powder is relatively dissolved, combine the liquid from your sealed container, the remaining 4 ounces of water, and the sugar in a saucepan and slowly bring the heat up to a light simmer. Whisk to incorporate, remove from the heat, and let cool before bottling and storing in the refrigerator. If, after your gum syrup has cooled, it appears too thick and is too difficult to use, fret not. Simply add a little more water ½ ounce at a time until you've reached the desired consistency.

DRINKING WITH FIRE

Now that the fire of inspiration is burning, let's look at all the different ways we can harness fire and smoke to benefit our drinking experience. There are a number of ways to add a smoky, campfire flavor to your cocktails, including:

* Charring ingredients to caramelize them.

* Smoking ingredients to impart an unmistakeable, aromatic new layer of flavor..

* "Campfire cooking," or cooking foil-wrapped ingredients right in a burning hot fire to concentrate their flavors.

* Drying herbs over a fire for a subtle hint of smoke.

* Using a small hand-held torch to toast spices or char herbs for garnish.

* Smoking a drink to order on a plank of wood.

One of the most glorious and exotic fruits of the cocktail world, the pineapple, happens to be one of the most well-suited to manipulation over an open flame. Charring the flesh of a pineapple helps to caramelize the sugars and intensify the flavors. Once caramelized and cooled, charred pineapple makes for delicious infusions into syrups and spirits, and even shines as a side dish, especially with pork dishes. A staple of the classic, pre-prohibition cocktail world, Pineapple Gomme, or Pineapple Gum Syrup, is a rich syrup flavored with pineapple and thickened with gum arabic, otherwise known as acacia powder, which is made from the hardened tree sap of the African acacia tree. Gum syrups originally became popular with bartenders and customers in the 1800s due to their uncanny ability to make cheap whiskey taste luxurious and give it a velvety texture. Acacia powder is a natural hydrocolloid like the ubiquitous xanthan gum, and essentially gives a cocktail a gentle "push" to

CHARRED PINEAPPLE-ROSEMARY GUM SYRUP

1 pineapple, top and bottom cut off,
halved lengthwise, leaving the rind on
(save the trimmed pieces for garnish
and for Tepache, page 228)

10 cloves

Small pinch of salt

2 sprigs of rosemary

Gum Syrup (page 219), cold

1 star anise pod

About an hour ahead of time, get your fire going to build up some coals, which you'll need to get a nice char on your pineapple. For this recipe, aim for medium heat; you should be able to hold your hand 5 inches above the grilling grate comfortably for 4 to 6 seconds.

You'll want a nice bed of coals below your grilling grate, leaving a little space surrounding the grates for the slowly burning wood to impart some smoke flavor on the pineapple. Stud each half of the pineapple's flesh with 5 cloves. Toss a little salt ("Salt Bae"-style, you know you want to) onto the pineapples as well.

Using tongs, place both halves of the pineapple flesh side down on the grilling grate, which should be sitting a few inches over the hot coals. Place the rosemary sprigs over the top of the pineapple rinds to pick up some smoke off the fire and give some pleasant aroma to the surround-ings. Feeling at one with the elements yet? Leave the pineapple to cook undisturbed for 3 to 4 minutes; remove the rosemary to use in a bit for the infusion, then check

continued →

the flesh side. If your fire is ripping hot, it may only take 5 minutes or so for the pineapple to become charred and for the sugars in the fruit to get nice and caramelized, or it could take up to 15 minutes. That's what can be so fun (and also challenging) about cooking over an open flame—it's no exact science, it just takes practice and trial and error. Once your pineapple is softening and browned on the flesh, it's ready to come off. For more of a smokey flavor, cook it a few more minutes for a more heavily charred surface. If you happen to overdo it, simply scrape off some of the darker colored charred flesh (like you would with burnt toast) and discard before you infuse the pineapple into the syrup.

Remove the pineapple from the grill and set aside until cool enough to handle. Remove the flesh from the rind by scooping it out with a spoon or cutting it off with a knife. Reserve the rind for another use (it has flavor, too!), chop the flesh into 2-inch segments, and place the flesh in the cold gum syrup. Add the star anise pod and the smoked rosemary to the syrup mixture, stir a few times, cover, and set in the refrigerator to infuse for 2 days, tasting the mixture after 1 day to see how the flavors are melding. If the rosemary is too strong, remove it. If there's too much char flavor, remove any charred bits and leave in the caramelized pineapple chunks. After 2 days, strain your syrup, bottle, and keep it in the fridge for one month. You now have a delicious elixir in your arsenal! With this beautiful potion, we're going to make two different cocktails that will allow the pineapple flavor to shine. First, we're going to combine the tiki classic The Jungle Bird (the only significant original tiki drink to come out of the 1970s) with the Kingston Negroni (a rum Negroni variation).

THE JUNGLE
NEGRONI

I ounce Plantation Pineapple Rum

I ounce Campari

¾ ounce Cocchi Torino Sweet Vermouth

¼ ounce Charred Pineapple-Rosemary Gum Syrup
(page 221)

I teaspoon fresh pineapple juice

3 drops saline solution
(I part water, I part salt, stirred to combine)

I sprig of rosemary, for garnish

2 pineapple fronds, for garnish

Fill a mixing glass three-quarters full with ice. Add the rum, Campari, vermouth, gum syrup, pineapple juice, and saline solution and stir until well chilled. Strain into an old fashioned glass over ice. Swipe the rosemary sprig back and forth on the sides of the glass a few times to release some of the oils onto the glass, then garnish the drink with the rosemary and pineapple fronds. If you happen to be an absinthe fan (bless you) try a different, boozier take on this drink by substituting absinthe for the teaspoon of pineapple juice. You'll notice how silky the mouthfeel is and how much easier it is to drink.

glide down the gullet smoothly. I'm a huge believer in gum syrups; they are probably the easiest way to take your home bar setup to the next level. You can use gum syrup in everything from an old fashioned to a daiquiri or margarita, and you will notice the difference in texture and mouthfeel in any cocktail you make with it. So before we get to charring our pineapple over an open fire, let's make a basic gum syrup recipe (see page 219), which can serve as the base for any flavored gum syrup you can dream up. The one I've always used is adapted from Jeffrey Morgenthaler, the cocktail savant from Seattle.

Now that we've got silky smooth deliciousness at our disposal, we're going to light a fire and flavor things up with some Charred Pineapple-Rosemary Gum Syrup. How you want to harness your fire is up to you—just don't get careless and set your house on fire. Be mindful of fire restrictions in your area and be careful using fire on a windy day. Unlike pineapple and rum, fire and wind don't mix well. Whether you're making your fire in the fireplace or on a simple grill in your backyard, you'll need some grilling grates to cook your pineapple on. When it comes to wood, I use all natural, cured (dried for at least a year) hickory, but other cooking woods like post oak, mesquite, and cherry can work as well. Just be mindful of the fact that different woods impart different flavors. Hickory and post oak are the most unobtrusive and complementary woods to use for pineapple. Mesquite can impart a very strong smoke flavor to ingredients (often too strong and a little bitter), and cherry and applewood have those definitive fruit flavors ideal for, you guessed it, cherries and apples, in addition to pork and chicken.

For the next drink, to further accentuate the slightly smoky and herbaceous flavor of the Charred Pineapple-Rosemary Gum Syrup (see page 221), we're going to use a blend of mezcal and tequila to make a margarita variation best for sipping by the fire and plotting your next vacation. To add a smoked flavor to the herb garnish,

THE FIRESIDE MARG

¾ ounce mezcal

1½ ounces tequila

¾ ounce lime juice

1 teaspoon orange juice

½ ounce Charred Pineapple-Rosemary Gum Syrup
(page 221)

1 teaspoon light agave

2 drops saline solution
(1 part water, 1 part salt, stirred to combine)

Yellow Chartreuse or Garden to Glass "Chartreuse"
(page 190), to rinse the glass

1 sprig of rosemary, for garnish

1 sprig of sage, for garnish

Pineapple fronds, for garnish

Fill a cocktail shaker with ice, add the mezcal, tequila, lime juice, orange juice, gum syrup, agave, and saline solution, and shake with ice until very cold. Add a capful of Chartreuse to a rocks glass and swirl to coat the inside of the glass. Discard the rest. "Roll" your ingredients, pouring everything, including the ice you shook with, into the Chartreuse-rinsed glass. Carefully torch the rosemary and sage sprigs with a little blast of fire from your handheld torch, then wave the herbs around to cool a bit. Garnish the drink with the cooled herbs and some pineapple fronds, and dream of palm trees and an ocean breeze.

"SMOKED" TEPACHE

1 pineapple,
very top and bottom removed
(fronds reserved for garnish),
rind and flesh cut into 2-inch segments,
plus any leftover rind or other
useable waste from the Charred
Pineapple-Rosemary Gum Syrup (page 221).

2 cups organic sugar

1 cinnamon stick,
crushed in a mortar and pestle
or on a towel with the bottom
of a cast-iron skillet

6 cloves

2 star anise pods

1 sprig of rosemary

1 tablespoon coriander

3 quarts water

Combine all the ingredients in a 4-quart container, stir to mix, and cover lightly with plastic wrap, allowing the brew to breathe. Set the container out at room temperature and check the brew after 24 hours. Skim off any white impurities that have floated to the top, and let the mixture ferment for another 24 hours, or until you see that it's mildly bubbling. Strain the mixture through cheesecloth, and serve over ice. If you don't drink all of it—and it's hard not to—keep your Tepache in a sealed container in the refrigerator and drink within a few days.

you'll need a handheld kitchen torch. This is one of the handiest tools you can have in your bar, restaurant, or home bar setup. Bonjour is one brand that's easy to find, but there are a host of different models on the market. Useful for more than just crème brûlée, a kitchen torch can help you toast spices very quickly and can release the flavors of certain hardy herbs like sage and thyme, which shine best when they are cooked. A few things to be careful of: First, never flame anything that's already in the glass, because you'll burn the glass and potentially the person's mouth who takes the first sip. If it's a cold drink, you also want to be careful not to raise the temperature of the drink too much by dropping a lit stick of rosemary in there. Give herbs a quick little char with the torch, then lightly shake them to decrease the temperature before using as a garnish. And of course, be careful not to burn your fingers, and the nerves therein!

Since we've still got the slightly smoky pineapple rind leftover from our Charred Pineapple syrup, and since we're running a low-waste operation here, we can look to our friends in Mexico for a simple, delicious, fermented pineapple drink known as Tepache (see page 226). This tropical brew is sold everywhere from bars to street carts, and is a refreshing, natural way to beat that south-of-the-border heat.

In addition to charring ingredients over a flame, you can also use the fire to "smoke" your syrups, infusions, and even assembled drinks. There are many different methods and tools available, but here we'll look at two basic ways to impart smoke, one focused on an ingredient, and the other on smoking an actual drink.

To "smoke" a syrup, the easiest and most natural method is to "trap and wrap" a burning, glowing ember into your pot of syrup. To do this, you'll need to have a natural, hot, outdoor fire burning (ideally using aged hickory or oak wood, though cherry or applewood

SMOKED MAPLE-
SAGE SYRUP

I quart maple syrup
(any good, natural maple syrup will do,
no Mrs. Buttersworth here)

A few sprigs of sage,
either fresh or dried over a fire

I ember from a natural-wood fire

Combine the maple syrup and sage in an 8-quart pot, leaving plenty of room for your burning ember, and place the pot near your fire. Lay out a piece of plastic wrap large enough to cover the pot, taking care to keep it stretched so it doesn't get bunched up. Tear off a few extra sheets and set them nearby (not on top of each other, they'll stick!) in case you need a little more to completely seal in the smoke. Wearing gloves and using tongs, choose a burning ember around 4 inches by 4 inches in size, carefully snatch it from the fire, and quickly drop it into the pot. The moment you drop the ember into the pot of syrup it will begin to smoke fiercely, so grab your already-prepped plastic wrap and completely wrap the pot to seal in the smoke. Resist the temptation to smell or taste the syrup for at least an hour. After an hour, take off the plastic wrap and carefully taste the syrup. If the smoke flavor is to your liking, simply strain out the ember through cheesecloth, bottle, and refrigerate for up to 2 months. If you want more smoke flavor, try adding another ember from the fire, re-wrapping the pot very quickly, and letting it smoke for another 45 minutes to an hour. Again, the most important part of this experiment is to wrap the syrup and trap in the smoke as soon as you can. If the initial blast of smoke evaporates into the air without being trapped in the syrup, you won't get much of a smoky flavor. The most delicious use of this syrup, aside from lathering it all over pancakes, is in a Manhattan riff, best sipped on a crisp autumn night.

SMOKED MAPLE-SAGE
MANHATTAN

2 ounces rye whiskey or bourbon

¾ ounce Cocchi Torino Sweet Vermouth

¼ ounce Smoked Maple-Sage Syrup
(page 228)

I bar spoon (⅛ ounce)
Garden to Glass Nocino (page 39)
or Nux Alpina Nocino (black walnut liqueur)

2 drops saline solution
(I part water, I part salt, stirred to combine)

3 dashes Angostura bitters

I orange twist, for garnish

I sage leaf,
lightly torched to awaken the aroma,
for garnish

Combine the whiskey, vermouth, syrup, nocino, saline solution, and bitters in a mixing glass and fill ¾ of the way with ice. Stir until well chilled and ice cold, 30 to 45 seconds. Strain into a coupe and garnish with the orange twist and sage.

would also work well), from which to take a red-hot ember. You'll also need to have a large pot, tongs, gloves, and plastic wrap on hand. What's fun about smoking maple syrup is, you are essentially returning the syrup back to the environment that it was created in: fire. Natural maple syrup is made by boiling the sap from the maple tree, which is relatively thin and watery, over a very hot fire. The sap gets concentrated, most of the water evaporates out, and you're left with thick, delicious syrup. It takes around 40 gallons of sap to make 1 gallon of syrup. The fact that it is "forged in the fire" makes it such a perfect candidate for this smoking method. In simple terms, grade A maple syrup is a little lighter and more nuanced than grade B syrup, but the grading system does not indicate that one is better than the other. I tend to like grade B for cocktails since it is slightly bolder in flavor, and I'm probably going to be drinking it with some bold spirits, like bourbon or rye whiskey. The key here is to use natural maple syrup, foregoing anything that includes high-fructose corn syrup.

With the fire still burning, it's the perfect time to point out that using fire to manipulate ingredients and concentrate flavors is a great way to get creative with fall and winter root vegetable bounty. It can be as simple as using the "campfire" method of cooking, touted by everyone from the Boy Scouts to Cracker Barrel, by wrapping your ingredients in tin foil, tossing them in the middle of a blazing fire, and fishing out a perfectly roasted vegetable 30 minutes later. One of the best-suited ingredients for this method is beets. With their tough exterior and rock-solid anatomy when mature, beets don't yield their delicious hearts very easily. Once fully cooked, though, red beets have a pleasant, earthy, aromatic sweetness, which is why nearly every restaurant in the country seems to have a beet salad on the menu. Golden beets have a milder, gentler taste and a sunshine-like soft golden color that makes them perfect when you want a milder taste in a beverage, or are looking to avoid the intense color of red beets. Both are

FIRE-ROASTED
BEET MEZCAL

3 to 4 red beets
(or yellow beets, for a softer
gold color and milder flavor),
tops removed and reserved

Kosher salt

3 to 4 teaspoons grapeseed oil
(or other mildly flavored cooking oil)

2 (750 ml) bottles of mezcal

Build a blazing hot fire using properly aged, all-natu-ral wood like hickory (which is perfect for the slightly smoky mezcal), oak, cherry, or applewood (remem-ber that each wood will impart a different flavor on the final product). Wearing gloves, wash the beets and peel them using a vegetable peeler or Y peeler. Spread out one sheet of tin foil for each beet that is big enough to wrap the beet completely. Place each beet on a piece of tin foil, lightly salt it, brush with a teaspoon or so of grapeseed oil, and completely wrap it with the tin foil. This will help lock in some mois-ture as the beets roast in the fire. As plenty of coals begin to form in the fire, toss your beets into the center of the blaze, throw a fresh log or two on, and sit back and taste the spirit you're infusing the beets into. Think about all the different flavor affinities and possibilities you'll have at your fingertips.

continued →

After 35 to 45 minutes, depending on how hot the fire is, snatch your beets with tongs and put them on a plate or tray to cool down. If they're ready, you should be able to feel some give when you squeeze the beets with your tongs. Since it is so thin, tin foil radiates away most of its heat relatively quickly, so you should be able to peel away some of the foil after a minute or so and check the beets for doneness. You want them to have some give, but not to be too mushy. If they don't appear to have been cooked enough, wrap them back in the tin foil and place them back in the fire for another 5 to 15 minutes. When the beets are done and have cooled enough to handle, carefully unwrap them and place them on a plate (you may not want to use a cutting board since the beets and their juices could stain it). Quarter the beets and place them in a 6-quart container with the mezcal. Stir to combine, cover, and let the infusion sit in a cool, dark place away from sunshine for 2 days. Taste after the initial 48-hour period and see if the flavors of the beets have blended with the mezcal. If you're pleased with the flavor, strain and bottle and use within 2 months. The color of the mezcal will now be a bright fuchsia, and will impart this beautiful color into any drink you make with it. Try this crazy-colorful sour:

BEET MEZCAL SOUR

1½ ounces Fire-Roasted Beet Mezcal

½ ounce simple syrup (or try an herbaceous,
vegetal syrup like cucumber (page 144)
or celery (page 150)

½ ounce lime juice

¼ ounce orange juice

¼ ounce Cynar
(an amaro made from artichokes)

I egg white

2 drops saline solution
(I part water, I part salt, stirred to combine)

Black pepper and beet greens, for garnish

Combine the mezcal, simple syrup, lime juice, orange juice, cynar, egg white, and saline solution in a shaker and mime shake without ice to begin to incorporate the egg white. Add a few large pieces of ice and shake vigorously until your arm gets tired. Strain into a coupe glass, allowing the foam on the top of the drink to settle before garnishing. To garnish, gently set 3 small beet leaves on top, then crack a small amount of black pepper over the top of the drink.

NOTE: To kick up the smoke flavor for this drink, add a teaspoon of Laphroaig 10-year scotch or another peaty scotch—but this variation is for smoky-drink-heads only.

amazing in their own right, but I prefer the red beets for their juice and earthy, French-wine-like aroma. They take to splashes of acid very well, whether from a squeeze of lemon or a tangy vinaigrette, and go well with everything from cheese to lettuce to beef short ribs. For our purposes, they are amazing for imparting color to infusions, and the juice doubles as a show-stopping color accent and a Bloody Mary secret ingredient (page 155). Think of all the acidic elements that go into a Bloody Mary, from hot sauce to lemon juice to tomato juice. A splash of beet juice in a Bloody Mary mix not only helps to deepen its magenta hue, it also gives the resulting drink more balance and complexity, contributing that earthy, rich aroma and subtly sweet flavor.

The spirits best-suited for use with beets are the vegetal, earthy mezcals and tequilas of Mexico. A mezcal margarita with a splash of beet juice thrown in belies its beautiful pink-purple hue with a punchy, bold powerhouse flavor that'll make you wonder why you hadn't thought of it before. With Fire-Roasted Beet Mezcal at your disposal, you'll never be at a loss for color or bold flavor for your cocktails. The roasted beets can even be made in your fireplace. You'll need gloves, tongs, and tin foil for roasting the beets (see page 231).

We've dealt with harnessing fire and smoke to infuse bold flavors into the individual components of a drink, such as syrups and spirits. Now we'll look at a method for "smoking" an actual drink itself, using the Polyscience Smoking Gun, a tool that is much easier to use than it sounds. The Smoking Gun is essentially a cooking bong without water (but yes, we will use herbs, man). It uses an internal fan to push the smoke out of its chamber or, for our purposes, out through a tube attachment and into the glass. There are different "smoking chips" available specifically for this tool, which come in small jars and are ready to use right away. You can also use any naturally cured wood you have around, such as the hickory we've used for our other recipes. All you do is put some small, broken-up pieces of wood, or the smoking chips, into the chamber of the Smoking Gun, light them with your hand-held torch, turn the gun on, and as the smoke filters through the tube, you let the smoke fill the empty glass you'll be drinking out of, then turn the glass over onto a plank of wood or a plate, trapping the smoke in the glass while you prepare the drink—let's say an old fashioned. When you're ready to pour the drink into the glass, turn the smoking glass over and pour the drink in as the smoke lifts out of the glass. You can accentuate the smokiness and add a layer of orange by flaming an orange peel over the glass, using a match and squeezing the orange oil over the top of the glass.

Another way to utilize fire and smoke in your Garden-to-Glass drinking experience is to dry your late-summer or fall herbs over a small fire. This enhances their flavors and can allow you to impart a little smoke on everything from teas and syrups to cordials, vinegars, and shrubs. Say you have a brand of mezcal that you like but wish was a tad smokier and more interesting for a cocktail you have in mind. Whether you have a fire going in the fireplace or outside in the fire pit, simply hang some rosemary near the fire, far enough away that it's not cooking, just picking up the dry air from the fire, and let it hang there for 6 to 8 hours. Once it cools, add it to your infusion for smoky, herbaceous deliciousness. These smoke-dried herbs are also great for infusing into honey or maple syrup. Smoked maple old fashioned anyone? And as we look ahead further into winter, drying herbs and tincturing them can help you use those herbal flavors all through the colder months.

HERBS: DRY 'EM IF YOU'VE GOT 'EM

Drying herbs and tincturing them is a way to use herbal flavors from the fall herb harvest all winter long. Tinctures are basically concentrated extracts that use alcohol as the solvent to extract the flavor and preserve it. I like to use a blend of fresh and dried herbs in tinctures, to capture a fuller flavor that represents the different stages of growth that the plant goes through. I prefer to lean more heavily on fresh herbs for their flavor and aromatic effects, and use dried in small amounts as a way to add structure and depth of flavor. You can also blend different tinctures together to create your own custom bitters blends, a practice that many commercial bitters companies, like Bittermen's, use to this day. You can't, however, use powdered herbs in tinctures.

While many herbalists use pure grain alcohol at 190 proof, some prefer 100 proof vodka, which offers a less astringent taste and allows you to showcase the ingredient more in a cocktail by using more of the tincture. If you're using hardy or dry botanicals and need to squeeze every bit of flavor out of them, 190 proof can be beneficial because the higher the alcohol content, the more flavor will be extracted. I generally prefer 100 proof vodka for my tinctures because I'm usually satisfied with the amount and freshness of whichever ingredient I'm using in the tincture. And you don't necessarily have to use vodka: If you know you'll be making a rum drink with the mint tincture that you're making, you can use some of the stronger rums, like Wray and Nephew Overproof, Smith and Cross, or Plantation OFTD (which originally stood for "Oh Fuck, That's Delicious," though they won't tell you that). These strong, delicious rums can be great for tincturing hard spices like cloves, cinnamon, nutmeg, and star anise. There are old "colonial bitters" recipes going back hundreds of years that used strong overproof rums as the solvent, so there's definitely some precedent for the idea. Strong overproof whiskey is another great solvent to use, if

RYE SAGE TINCTURE

1 cup fresh sage
¼ cup dried sage leaves
100 proof or stronger rye whiskey
(I like Rittenhouse)

Fill a 32-ounce Mason jar with as much fresh sage as you can, without packing it. Add the dried sage and fill the jar with whiskey. Add the seal and cap, shake vigorously to incorporate, and set the jar in a cool, dark place for 2 weeks, shaking every few days. Strain the mixture through cheesecloth and bottle in a small dropper bottle. Store at room temp and use within a year.

you happen to be making a tincture that you feel would be a great addition to a whiskey drink. Here's an example of a sage tincture, using rye whiskey as the solvent. This formula can be adapted to other tincture ideas.

In addition to using a few drops of your tinctures right in a cocktail, you can also use an atomizer to spray the aromatic tincture over the drink right before serving or drinking it. This sends the full aroma of the tincture over the entire glass. Since what you smell is what you taste, this can add a huge layer of flavor to a drink, especially in those crucial first few sips of a cocktail.

As the holidays roll in, with all their excess, glory, hangovers, family strife, crowded airports, busy restaurants, and delayed flights, there's one thing that can help you make it through: you guessed it, a cocktail! Carrying a small cocktail kit on an airplane is a fun way to take the Garden–to-Glass ethos to the skies. Using a small metal card case or one of those small little packs used to carry essential oils, you can carry *most* of the essential items needed for a good cocktail on a plane. Here's what you'll pack:

* 1 dropper bottle of Rye Sage Tincture (page 237)

* 1 dropper bottle of Angostura or other aromatic bitters

* 1 dropper bottle of Garden to Glass "Chartreuse" (page 190—it's medicine, right?)

* 1 dropper bottle of sweet vermouth

* 2 sprigs of thyme or sage

For your in-flight cocktail, all you'll need to do is order an airplane bottle of the spirit of your choice—gin, rum, reposado tequila, or whiskey—a cup of ice, and a packet of sugar. This cocktail has the ability to steel the nerves, settle the stomach, and soften the heart.

BOOZY IN THE SKIES

1 airplane bottle gin, rum,
reposado tequila, or whiskey

10 drops Rye Sage Tincture (page 237)

10 drops Angostura bitters

10 drops Garden to Glass "Chartreuse" (page 190)

20 to 30 drops sweet vermouth

½ teaspoon sugar

Thyme or sage leaves, for garnish

In your small plastic cup filled with ice, combine the spirit of your choice with the tincture, bitters, Chartreuse, and vermouth. Stir the drink together, adding the sugar, and garnish with the thyme leaves. Sure, you may get a cursory, judgey look from your fellow passengers, but hey, at least you didn't bring Popeye's chicken on the plane, stinking up the whole cabin. You actually made your whole row smell like a garden, and if anyone else wants one, you've got enough in the dropper bottles to share. It is the holidays, after all.

When you return back home, needing a vacation from vacation, and your plants are either falling over or covered in pine straw mulch just waiting for another day in the sun, remember every new season gives you something new to grow. There is always a new plant to seek out and grow, or a new spot to try and grow something— maybe over there, by the shed, in that spot where you never knew rhubarb could grow. There may even be a sunny spot in the house to start a few plants earlier than you thought. The next thing you know, the cycle is starting over again, even though it truly never stops. Plants look, feel, and taste different throughout their growth cycles, and there's nothing more satisfying than seeing your little seedlings pop up, ready for another shot in the garden come springtime. I'll glance at a shoot of mint coming up in February and think, "I wonder how many drinks will be made using that one plant." Sharing what you grow, as Tom Maddox pointed out, is a way to connect us all. And the more things you grow, the more you'll realize how connected everything is. The pollinators of the world need us just like the plants we grow need pollinators. So put some seeds into a pot, give it some love, sunshine, and water, and when it's ready, get it in the ground and watch it grow. If it doesn't work, try something else, or try doing it just a little bit differently. You'll find that all the love you put into your garden will come back to you as wisdom, inspiration, peace, and the interconnected joy of every living thing on this planet.

INDEX

Page numbers in italics represent illustrations.

ACKNOWLEDGEMENTS

Thank you: Stephanie Bowman and everyone at Turner
Publishing, Christine McKnight, Mark and Cheryl Wolf,
Matt, Lisa and Anabelle Wolf, Don and Cathy Barnett,
Christine and Rob, John and Kali, Bob and Ashley
Souder, Peter Eugene Edwards, Bryce McCloud,
Sean Brock, G Brown, Matt Campbell, Kenneth Dedmon
and everyone at Husk, Jessica Backhus, Kevin King,
Jessica Machen, Brian Baxter, Nate Leonard,
Chris, Tracy and Winston from White Squirrel Farm, Tom
Maddox, Chris Bennett, Stephen Polcz,
Hrant and Liz Arakelian, Nick Hood, Rory O'Connell,
Amie Hartley-Leonard, Kenny Lyons, David Howard,
Ashley Wood, Caitlin DeMichele, Nick Drohan,
Nick Thaxton, Andy Mumma, Morgan McGlone,
Lisa Donovan, Michael Eades, Ali Besten, Will Motley,
Patrick Goodspeed, Tracy Ardoin-Jenkins, Leah Smith,
Taryn Breen, Graham Fuze, Kyle Simmons,
Andy and Karen Little, Colby Rasavong, Madeline
Crowley, Adam Morgan, Brodekine Schmeilha,
Inglewood Public Library, and David Berman